Don't Tell Anyone Where You Are Going:

*My Adventures Growing Up in Iowa
from 1893 to 1968*

By

Sylvia Glendenning Lay

With Douglas Lay

Don't Tell Anyone Where You Are Going:
My Adventures Growing Up in Iowa from 1893 to 1968

© Douglas Lay 2016

DEDICATION

To Sylvia:

your narrative

has finally made it out

of the darkness of the cellar

into the light of the new century.

INTRODUCTION

This is a story about an explorer...

Not Columbus, who sailed over 4,000 miles to reach the new world, nor Magellan who covered over 42,000 miles to circumnavigate the globe, nor Neil Armstrong, who in Apollo 11, traveled nearly a million statue miles to reach the moon and back.

No, this is a story about a four-foot eleven-inch woman who traveled, over a 40-year period, less than twenty miles within only one county in southern Iowa during the first third of the 20th century.

This is a story about a woman who survives, at the age of five, a near death childhood illness but whose younger brother does not;

a woman who is robbed of a loving relationship with her father because of his accidental death shortly after her birth;

a woman who gains eight new family members after her mother remarries;

a woman who mourns the deaths of family and friends from not one but from two World Wars;

a woman who struggles to earn a living with her husband from farming during the great depression and the devastating dust bowl;

a woman who wrestles with depression without access to the numerous treatments afforded people today;

a woman who lives with no security of home ownership, moving 34 times in over 40 years;

a woman who raises two sons who graduate from college although she only attends high school for two years;

a woman who has 12 grandparents, 84 aunts and uncles, 1 step-father, 1 step-sister, 2 half-brothers, 5 half-sisters, over 100 first cousins, five grandchildren, and nine-great grandchildren;

a woman who lives the first twenty years of her life single, then remains married to the same man for 55 years and then lives the next 22 years as a widow;

a woman who lives out her Christian faith that stretches over 80 years;

a woman who is known by her friends as Sylvia Glendenning Lay;

a woman who is known to me simply as *Gram Lay*. This is her story, written by her own hand, of her adventures growing up in Southern Iowa from 1893 to 1968.

The Genesis of Her Story

In 1965, Robert Lay, Sylvia's oldest son, approached her to record her life growing up in Ringgold County in southern Iowa from her birth in 1893 to 1935, her move to Des Moines, Iowa in 1935, her move to Valley Junction in 1939, and then a brief recollection of her life in West Des Moines from 1949 to 1968.

So Sylvia, my grandmother, wrote out her life story, by hand, and my uncle meticulously typed out, on a manual typewriter with carbon paper, multiple copies.

SYLVIA GLENDENNING LAY[1]

```
4-8-67
                Sylvia Glendenning Lay      Febr. 1965.
        The following written for me by my Mother;
        I was born on a farm south of Mt. Ayr, Iowa, Oct. 31, 1893.
    My Mother was Mary Ollie Steadman Glendenning.  My Father was
    Robert Glendenning and Mother's Father was James Samuel Steadman.
    My Father's Father was Peter Glendenning.  The two Grandparents lived
    on farms about one-fourth mile apart.  Grandpa Steadman had a
    croquet ground in the orchard and the two of them played croquet
    for amusement.
        When I was two years old my Father passed away, leaving Mother a
    widow at the age of 22 years with a baby to raise.  For one year after
    his death, we spent our time between the two Grandparents. My
    Grandmother Glendenning had been dead for a few years and Aunt
    Sylvia kept house for Grandpa. (Grandma Steadman was alive then
    and for many years).  While I was too young to remember, Grandpa
    Glendenning and my Aunt and Uncles moved to Kalispell, Montana.
        When I was three years old, Mother married Peter Rush.  He had
    a daughter, Fairy, one year and one week older than I.  We grew up
    as sisters.  When I was five, the folks moved to Montana to
    Columbia  Falls--not too far from Kalispell. Think Grandpa
    Glendenning lived on a farm not too far away.
        Aunt Ollie and Uncle Curt Abarr lived out there too.  Lela Abarr
    and I went to the timber with Grandpa and he made each of us a little
    rolling pin out of wood.  Fairy and I started to school.  I remember
    I was told the first day of school to not come to school.  I was
    too young.  I remember I was disappointed for Fairy and I had always
    been able to go together and do the same things.  We only lived in
    Montana six months. The folks didn't like it out there.
        So we moved back to Iowa. Moved in a small house southeast of
    Delphos. We were in the Delphos school district.  Fairy and I walked to
    school.  Was a long walk.  We had to pass a large orchard with no
    buildings around.  Belonged to old Mr. Fisher.  So many apples on
    the ground so we filled our dinner pails.  When we got home, we got
    a lesson on stealing that I will never forget.  We didn't know we
    were stealing. We were just getting some apples to eat.
        The folks had a baby boy before we went to Montana.  While we
    were living in the first house we moved after coming back, the baby
    and I had the Black Measles.  Dad's nephew came from Oklahoma and came
    down with them.  This was in summer time, I think.  My hair came out s
    bad they cut my curls all off.  Fairy was at her Grandma Pratt's
    when we were exposed so she didn't get them.  I think it was tha
```

---

[1] This is a picture of page one of the actual 1965 typed manuscript of Sylvia's narrative. This edition included 19 total pages.

Three years later, Robert asked her to produce a second narrative; so she wrote again in 1968—a retelling of the same story from 1965 but with several additional episodes.

For the next nineteen years, it is unclear what had happened to the two narratives, but in 1987, Robert wrote a postscript to her story and apparently sent a copy of the narratives to his brother, Paul Lay, Sylvia's younger son, my father. Three years later, my uncle would pass away.

After my grandmother's death in 1991, my father received all of her possessions as the executor of her estate. Included in her personal items were over a hundred photos, dozens of paper clippings of obituaries, documents, and the two carbon paper narratives written by her over 25 years earlier.

For the next 20 years, my grandmother's story laid dormant in an old box in a cigar smoked-filled basement at my father's home in Carroll, Iowa. Sylvia's story was discovered in January of 2011, several days after my father's death, while I was going through dozens and dozens of boxes in his basement.

It was quite the discovery!

At first, I re-typed both narratives and then over the summer of 2011, I combined both stories into one coherent story. Without the assistance of any living relatives from the story, I began the tedious process to research the dozens and dozens of people mentioned by utilizing numerous genealogical web sites, other family documents, obituaries, and cemetery records. After over three years, all of Sylvia's family members were identified, not only those referred to in the story, but all 12 grandparents, 84 aunts and uncles, over 100 first cousins, and the Lay family tree back to the 1600's and the Glendenning family history back to the 1300's.

At the same time, I attempted to identify all of the locations of the farms where she had lived and the schools and churches she had attended. Using a hand-written map produced by Robert; farm maps from 1894, 1915, and 1930; and Google Earth, all of the locations were found and identified.

I made five trips to Ringgold County over the next three years (June 2011; Oct 2011; Feb 2013; Oct 2013; Aug 2014) to locate each of the references in Sylvia's story along with photographing each site. On one trip in 2011, the county sheriff, after receiving several calls from concerned citizens, spent an hour tracking down a "stranger" taking pictures!

During the summer of 2014, the narrative was divided into chapters and then sub-divisions were added to each chapter. Although Sylvia did not organize her story around a particular order, her story did fit into a loose chronological structure, giving snap shots of her life. Except for a few minor editorial changes—grammar, spelling, and organization—this story appears exactly as Sylvia wrote nearly 50 years ago.

The original intention was to publish her story only for her living grandchildren (Karen, Thomas, Gary, Douglas, David) who still have fond memories of her and for her nine great-grandchildren (Lisa, Robbie, Amanda, Katie, Jennifer, Jessica, Tiffany, David, Priscilla), who although have limited memories of her, were all born before Sylvia passed away in 1991.

Yet, after spending the past four years engulfed in my grandmother's story, it occurred to me that her story might have a broader audience. She gives glimpses into a way of life that is profoundly contrasted with life today.

Sylvia's story reminds us that as we reconnect with our past, it lays a foundation for our future.

The Origin of the Title

When my grandmother was eighteen, she traveled, by train, over 1,500 miles to visit her grandpa Peter Glendenning in northern Montana, about 50 miles south of the Canadian border. Traveling alone, she left Delphos, Iowa in the spring of 1912, with a suitcase with several homemade dresses and advice from her aunt Jedi: "Don't talk to strangers" and "Don't tell anyone where you are going."

Although she would make two trips to Montana in her lifetime, Sylvia spent the first 42 years of her life living in one southern Iowa County, Ringgold County. She lived within only about a 120 square mile area, about the size of Des Moines and West Des Moines combined, yet she would move 32 times.[2]

---

[2] For a detailed description of each move, see Appendix A, *The Explorations of Sylvia Glendenning Lay / Time-Line:*

Sylvia lived nearly the first half of her 97 years of life on the move, quietly transitioning between the challenges of drawing a living from the land on the farm and finding employment in the small townships of southern Iowa.

She traveled in silence, without any fanfare, without any applause, without any recognition.

There wasn't time to tell everyone where she was going; there was work to do—five half-sisters and two half-brothers to help raise; a step-father to share the chores with on the farm; a classroom of children to teach in a two-room school house; a husband to support in the fields and in town; two young boys to raise; elderly family members to visit and help; numerous boarders to feed and provide for; countless quilts, dresses, and work clothes to sew and mend; hours of food gathering, preparing, and serving; trips to the cemetery to lay to rest two half-brothers, a father, several aunts, and grandparents; traveling to an out of town hospital by train to care for a dying husband; conferring with doctors miles away to seek treatment for "her nerves"; and finding the time each week to hitch up the wagon and trek down unpaved rural roads to worship her God.

Sylvia wasn't an explorer traveling to exotic locations around the globe, making historical discoveries and reporting her findings in academic journals, telling the world where she had been.

No. She was too busy living out her walk with the Lord to tell anyone where she was going. She lived out her faith in the Lord as she journeyed for nearly a century, trusting the Lord that as long as He knew where she was going, she didn't need to tell anyone—until now.

As you walk alongside Sylvia on her journey through the rolling prairies of southern Iowa over 100 years ago, I hope you will see an amazing young early American explorer—Sylvia Glendenning Lay—my grandmother.

The Foundation for the Layout

Each chapter begins with a summary of Sylvia's life during a specific time frame.

1893-1991 at the end of this book.

Then each chapter provides a snapshot of her life, written by Sylvia, displayed in the *Goudy Old Style* font. Included in each chapter are background sections explaining and expounding on material Sylvia mentions in her story, written by me and displayed in the *Calibri Light* font to distinguish it from Sylvia's writings.

There are several sections written by my uncle, Robert Lay, and they are indicated so. Nearly all of the photos of people are from Sylvia's collection, with a small number of pictures supplemented from other referenced sources. I took nearly all of the photos of the farms, the schools, the churches, and the cemeteries on a number of visits to Ringgold county.

It is with great joy and expectation that I present my grandmother's adventures as an early 20th century explorer on her 122nd birthday.

Douglas Lay
October 31, 2015

Table of Contents

Chapter 1   Go West, Young Woman (1912)   1

Chapter 2   Stormy Beginnings (1893-1899)   11

Chapter 3   City of "Sisters" (1899-1902)   23

Chapter 4   Grandpa Memories (1902-1905)   33

Chapter 5   Let the Angels Rejoice (1905-1908)   47

Chapter 6   From Student to Teacher (1908-1913)   57

Chapter 7   Wedding Bells (1914)   69

Chapter 8   Up on the Farm (1914-1916)   75

Chapter 9   Change is Coming (1916-1919)   87

Chapter 10   Mystery of Life (1919-1927)   101

Chapter 11   On the Move (1927-1935)   117

Chapter 12   Don't Look Back (1935-1939)   131

Chapter 13   The War Years (1939-1948)   141

Chapter 14   Marriage and Death (1949-1968)   153

Chapter 15   Life After John (1969-1991)   159

Epilogue   A Godly Woman (1893-1991)   167

Acknowledgement		175
Appendix A	Time Line: 1893 to 1991	177
Appendix B	Grandparents	180
Appendix C	Aunts and Uncles	181
Appendix D	Glendenning Family Tree	184
Appendix E	Lay Family Tree	188
Appendix F	Rush Family Tree	193
Appendix G	Five Generations	194
Editor	Douglas Lay	210

1

GO WEST, YOUNG WOMAN

1912

Although Sylvia lived almost 98 years in Iowa, she would live about six months in northern Montana at the age of five when her parents moved to Kalispell to live with Sylvia's grandparents. Then at the age of 18, she would spend several weeks visiting her grandpa Glendenning in Montana for the last time. She recounts her two-day train ride from Iowa to Montana; her visit to Spokane, Washington to see her Aunt Sylvia Steadman, her mother's sister, and their family; and her visit with Uncle Claude, her grandfather's son, and the younger brother of Sylvia's father, Robert Glendenning.

Kalispell, Montana 1905[3]

[3] Picture courtesy of Dale Jones.

Don't Talk to Strangers

After school was out in the spring (1912), I decided to go visit my grandfather Glendenning who I hadn't seen since I was five years old. I wanted my cousin to go with me. She was teaching, too, but she wanted to wait a year. So mother and I made me some dresses, and I went to Montana. I had never taken a trip, so I was pretty green. Aunt Jeda[4] said,

"Don't talk to strangers" and "Don't tell anyone where you are going."

It took a couple of days to go. Once a man sat down by me just before the conductor came for the tickets. After the conductor had gone, the man said,

"Did you say you were going to Canada?"

"I didn't say."

Guess I thought he wanted to kidnap me! I had to change trains at Columbia Falls (photo below[5]), the town where I had lived about 14 years before. The only train going to Kalispell was like a bumpy wagon. It was in the night. A man, woman, and child seemed to be the only passengers.

Columbia Falls

---

[4] Aunt Jeda was Margaret Geneve (Anderson) Rush, the wife of Sirestus Marion Rush, the brother of Peter Rush, Sylvia's stepfather.
[5] Train station in Columbia Falls, Montana. 1905. Public domain picture.

UNION PACIFIC RAILROAD

Sylvia most likely left the Delphos railroad station (photo below[6]) and traveled northwest to Omaha, NE, and then traveled on the Union Pacific Railroad, west through Nebraska, Wyoming, and then northwest to Idaho, and then north to Butte, Montana. She most likely picked up another train north through Helena, Great Falls, Shelby, then west through Glacier Park and then south to Columbia Falls.

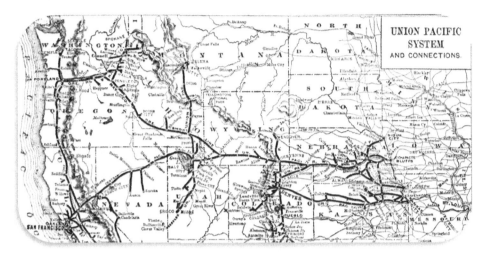

Sylvia mentions she changed trains in Columbia Falls to Kalispell. Columbia Falls was about 50 miles south of the Canadian border. If Sylvia were to travel the most direct route today from Delphos to Kalispell by car, it would take about 21 hours, a distance of 1,400 miles.

A Stranger on the Train

When we got to Kalispell, no one was there to meet me. I was so dumb; I didn't know what to do. I asked a couple who had been on the train with me if they knew P.C. Glendenning. The man said he knew where he lived, and they would show me. So dumb me, I went off with perfect strangers. We walked and then stopped at a house. The woman stayed there, and the man and I went on. When we finally reached Grandpa's house, we woke up Grandma. (Grandpa had remarried since I had last seen him). She said Grandpa had already met two trains and thought there wouldn't be another one until the morning. She wondered why I didn't go to a hotel. I never thought to go since I had never been to a hotel. I went to bed for the rest of

---

[6] Photo public domain.

the night. I had a very nice time; everyone was very nice to me.

Sylvia visits Sylvia

Grandma had a daughter my age.[7] She and Grandpa had a son, George, who was 7 years old. Grandpa was 75. I stayed a few days, and then I went on to Spokane, Washington to visit Aunt Sylvia and Uncle Abner[8]. I had seen her when I was eight years old. I wrote her when I was coming, but she didn't get my letter, so as usual, no one was there to meet me. We found my letter later in Grandpa's pocket. He had forgotten to mail it. Grandma said, "We won't tell him."

SYLVIA'S MOTHER
AND AUNTS

Back Row:
Mary Steadman
(Sylvia's Mother),
Alice Steadman

Front Row:
Fannie Steadman,
Hattie Steadman,
Sylvia Glendenning

---

[7] This may have been a daughter from a previous marriage. Sylvia's grandmother had a daughter with Peter Glendenning (Fern), but she was younger than Sylvia, not the same age.
[8] Aunt Sylvia Glendenning (Hooper) was the daughter of Sylvia's grandfather and his second wife, Louisa Hollingsworth. Aunt Sylvia was ten years older than her brother, Robert Glendenning, Sylvia's father. Aunt Sylvia was born in 1875, married Abner Hooper, and had one child, Paul Hooper, born in 1915. Aunt Sylvia died in 1950.

This time I arrived in daylight. I asked how to get to Hilliard, a place on the edge of Spokane. I was told what bus to take, and I had the street number, so I arrived o.k. I went to the door and knocked, but Aunt Sylvia didn't expect me that day. She thought I was selling something. She said,

"What can I do for you, girlie?"

Then it dawned on her who I was. She made me lie down on the cot to rest, and then she rushed over to her neighbors, dad and mom Falkerson, as she called them. They had to come over and meet me. I had a lovely time there. She made me hide when Uncle Abner came home. She wanted to surprise him. He could tell she was excited because when she had me come out of hiding, he said,

"I know it was something the way Babe acted."

They had a new lovely house. It didn't have the upstairs finished yet, and it had only one bedroom furnished. So Uncle Abner took a mattress, laid it on chairs some way, and slept on that while I slept with Aunt Sylvia.

The Single Artist

Uncle Claude [9] lived at a hotel between Kalispell and Spokane. He was a painter and was single. I had written him when I would be in his town and asked him to get on the train and go to Grandpa's with me. He couldn't that day, so he

---

[9] Uncle Claude was the son of Peter C Glendenning and Louise (Hollingsworth), Sylvia's grandparents. Uncle Claude was born on October 26, 1878 and died on January 4, 1943.

went to the station up the road and got a train. I wasn't expecting him there. He came through the train and recognized me. He hadn't seen me either since I was five. He said he couldn't go that day but wanted me to stop at his town and stay till the next day. So I got off. He took me to the hotel and got me a room, my very first room. He took me out to supper.

POSTCARD FROM PETER (UNCLE) CLAUDE GLENDENNING TO SYLVIA LAY

"My dear Niece: Your letter came today and I'll send you another card. I sent you one of these sometime ago but I guess you did not get it. I'll write to you in a few days. I would like to see you. Bye Bye, Your Uncle Claude. P. S. This is a hunting trip I took last fall. Did you get the other one I sent you?" (March 26, 1911)

Uncle Claude is second from the left

Canada Trip

The next morning, he rented a team and buggy and took me for a long drive, showing me the irrigating ditches. We were only 1.5 miles from Canada, but we didn't save time to go farther, or I would miss my train. I went back to Grandpa's that evening, and Uncle Claude came a few days later.

While he was there, we all went to the mountains. Grandpa had a carriage, so we drove to the edge of the mountains. Grandma fixed a lovely picnic lunch. Uncle Claude and I climbed up the mountain a little way, which was quite a thrill for me.

On the way back, we stopped at the cemetery where Aunt Ollie Abarr was buried (photo right[10]).

One day Fern[11] (Grandma's daughter) invited me to go with her class on a boat trip. The coward I was, I wouldn't go, so Fern stayed home with me.

Last Visit with Grandpa

I was gone from Iowa about three weeks. After I went home, I never saw Grandpa again. Before I arrived, the barn door had blown down on his head. He kept saying his head hurt when I was there. The next year, he passed away.

THE OBITUARY OF PETER CASSEL GLENDENNING[12]

"Glendenning departed this life at his home in Kalispell, Montana Wednesday, August 20, 1913. The funeral was held on Thursday at the M. E. church, Rev. Armstrong officiating. Interment being made in Fairview Cemetery on the east side of the river. Among the hymns rendered were 'It's not death to die' and 'Asleep in Jesus.'"

"The sermon was taken from the 16th Psalm, 15th verse. The deceased was a son of John and Elizabeth Glendenning, having been born in Rush County, Indiana, June 17, 1838, being at the time of his departure past 75 years of age. His grandfather, Henry Glendenning, had been a soldier in the War of 1812. His great grandfather was a native of Scotland but came to America when a young man and was a soldier in the Revolutionary War."

---

[10] Fairview Cemetery, Columbia Falls, Montana. Mary Olive Glendenning (Abarr) was born in 1862 and died on November 7, 1901. She was the sister of Sylvia's mother. Public domain picture.
[11] Fern Glendenning was Sylvia's aunt, about 10 years younger than Sylvia. Fern was one of two children by Peter Glendenning and his third wife, Eliza Carpenter. Fern's brother, George, was born in 1905.
[12] The obituary appeared in the paper in Montana in August of 1913.

"P.C. Glendenning's maternal grandfather, Elijah Carter, was a descendent of the noted Carter who engaged in the early Indian wars, Station, Tenn. in the early history and who built the Fort at Carter's of that commonwealth. P.C. Glendenning came to Gentry Co., MO with his parents in 1841 and reared in that community. He began preaching for the M.E. Church at the age of 35, and had continued preaching at intervals ever since until quite recently."

"He served four years in the Civil War as Corporal, Co. 1, 3rd Regiment, Missouri Militia. He was first married to Miss Sarah Ross in 1861. To them were born two children, John J. (James) and Mary Olive, both gone on before."

"Married again in 1866 to Louisa Hollingsworth. To them were born four children, Rev. T.E. Glendenning, Correctionville, Ia; Robert H. who died in Iowa in 1895; Mrs. Sylvia H. Hooper of Hillyard, Washington; and Claude of Columbia Falls, Montana. Married again to Mrs. Eliza A. Lines in 1904. To them was born one child, George O., now 8 years of age. His most excellent wife survives him also."

"Rev. Glendenning came to Flat Head some 16 years ago and bought a ranch on the east side where he resided until a few years ago when he felt that he could no longer lead the strenuous life of the ranch, so he rented it and came to Kalispell, Mont., where he bought a most beautiful home where he continued to live to the last. Rev. Glendenning was a man whom it was a pleasure to meet and converse with, always strewing words of kindness and cheer everywhere, and he will be sadly missed in the community."

"There is no death, the sun goes down, To rise upon some fairer shore, And there in Heaven's Jeweled Crown, To shine for evermore." --An Old Friend—

UNCLE PETER CLAUDE GLENDENNING

Sylvia's uncle, Peter Claude, was the youngest son of Sylvia's grandfather, Peter Glendenning and his second wife, Louisa Hollingsworth. Uncle Claude moved to Montana with his parents in 1899. In 1943, uncle Claude was killed in auto accident in Spokane, Washington. His obituary is below.[13]

"Peter Claude Glendenning was born October 26, 1878, in Mount Ayr [Ringgold Co.], Iowa. In 1899 Mr. Glendenning moved with his parents to the Flathead and was later united in marriage to Helen MacBain. To this union one son was born, Robert B., who is now in the armed forces. Mr. Glendenning was injured in an automobile accident in Spokane a few weeks ago, the result of which caused his death January 4,

---

[13]Daily Interlake Newspaper, Jan 5, 1943.

1943. Besides his wife and son, he is survived by his stepmother, Mrs. E.[Eliza] A. Glendenning of Columbia Falls; a half-brother, George, of Seattle, and a sister, Mrs. Sylvia Hooper. "

FAIRVIEW CEMETERY, COLUMBIA FALLS, MONTANA[14]

Left: Peter Cassel Glendenning (Sylvia's Grandfather)
Right: Robert Burton Glendenning (Sylvia's cousin; son of Peter Claude)
Flag: Peter Claude Glendenning (Sylvia's Great Uncle; son of Peter Cassel)

---

[14] Picture public domain.

2

STORMY BEGINNINGS

1893-1899

Sylvia's story begins on Halloween, October 31, 1893 on a farm owned by John S. Stedman, Sylvia's grandfather. By the time she had turned five, her life had already been filled with disappointment—first with the tragedy of death, then the uncertainty of the future, then the challenge of a new family, then the tragedy of death again, and then the uncertainty of the future again. Yet, she recounts that her first memory about her early life was not of the tragedies and uncertainties of life, but rather about a time her grandpa Glendenning, from Montana, showed her an act of kindness and love, an act she would still remember very fondly nearly 70 years later.

Blessing of Life

I was born Sylvia Geneva Glendenning in Ringgold County, Iowa, on a farm south of Mt. Ayr, Iowa, on October 31, 1893. My mother was Mary Ollie Steadman Glendenning, and my Father was Robert Glendenning.

James Steadman Farm[15]

Tragedy of Death

When I was two years old, my father, Robert Glendenning, passed away, leaving mother a widow at the age of 22 years with a baby to raise.

OBITUARY OF ROBERT H. GLENDENNING[16]

"Robert H. Glendenning was born in Gentry County, Missouri, August 12, 1868 and died at his home in Middle Fork Township on November 24, 1895 of brain trouble caused by injuries on the head received by being thrown from a horse several

---

[15] Sylvia was born on the farm of James Steadman, one of her father's farms, located southeast of Delphos in Middle Fork Township #1. The farm was west of 220th Ave. and south of 280th St. The location of the farm comes from a map made by Robert Lay, Sylvia's oldest son, made in 1971. See *Maps of the Farms* at the end of this chapter. (See *Ringgold County 1894 Iowa Historical Atlas*).

[16] Newspaper clipping from Sylvia Lay.

months ago."

"He came to Ringgold County with his parents, Rev. and Mrs. P.C. Glendenning, in the spring of 1875. He was married to Miss Olive Steadman, daughter of J. S. Steadman of Middle Fork Township, who with one child, a little daughter is left to mourn this loss. He also leaves a father, two brothers, and two sisters, his Mother having died June 28, 1890. He was a member of the Methodist Episcopal Church."

"The funeral services took place at Middle Fork chapel at 11 o'clock on Monday, conducted by Rev. Williams of Leon, after which the remains were interred in the cemetery [17] at that place. The bereaved wife and little daughter, who have lost a kind and affectionate husband and father, and also other relatives, have the sincere sympathy of a large number of friends."

MIDDLE FORK UNITED METHODIST CHURCH[18]

The Middle Fork United Methodist Church, dedicated in 1886, is located next to the Middle Fork cemetery (photo below).

[17] Robert Glendenning's headstone at Middle Fork Cemetery. Picture copyright by D. Lay.
[18] *Middle Fork United Methodist Church.* http://iagenweb.org/ringgold/church/files/ch-middleforkme.html.

Sylvia's grandmother, Della (Willey) Steadman, and grandfather, James Steadman, were original members of the church, as were Sylvia's great uncle and aunt, Mr. and Mrs. Thomas Glendenning. Sylvia's grandfather, P.C. Glendenning, assisted with the first revival meeting at the building in 1887. The work on the church was all donated by the congregation, and they raised the funding before the building was constructed, paying cash up front and allowing the people to never have to take out a mortgage.

Their motto was, "build it to last 100 years." The church is listed on the National Register of Historical Places and continues to conduct services today.

The Dueling Grandparents

For one year after his death, we spent our time between the two grandparents. My mother's father was James Samuel Steadman[19] and my father's father was Peter Glendenning.

Peter Glendenning Farm[20]

The two grandparents lived on farms about one-fourth mile apart. Grandpa Steadman had a croquet set in the orchard, and both grandfathers played croquet for amusement.

James Steadman Farm[21]

---

[19] James Steadman was born January 29, 1847 and died August 24, 1917.
[20] The Glendenning farm is in the Middle Fork Township #11 located east of Highway 169 and north of 300th St. (See *Ringgold County 1894 Iowa Historical Atlas*).
[21] The Steadman farm was in Middle Fork Township #3 and #10. The picture is looking east on 290th St. towards Highway 169. (See *Ringgold County 1894 Iowa Historical Atlas*).

Peter's wife, my grandmother Glendenning (Louisa Hollingsworth), had been dead for a few years, and Aunt Sylvia Glendenning kept house for grandpa Glendenning.

OBITUARY OF LOUISA (HOLLINGSWORTH) GLENDENNING[22]

"Sister Glendenning was religious from early childhood and early in life became identified with the M.E. church of which she continues a most worthy member until called to join the triumphant throng above. She had gifts of high order and was an excellent worker in the church, being always ready to give 'a reason of the hope that was within her' and to perform any service what was for God's glory. Many sleepless nights she spent by the bedside of the afflicted where her presence was always felt to be a blessing. Religion with her was not guesswork. She knew for herself that Christ had power on earth to forgive sin and to cleanse from all unrighteousness; she lived in the smile of his countenance."

MIDDLE FORK CEMETERY

Left:
Robert Glendenning's
gravestone (Sylvia's Father)

Right:
Louise (Hollingsworth)
Glendenning (Sylvia's
Grandmother)

"Glendenning remarked that he had lived with her 24 years and never knew her angry. She was a model house-keeper, a faithful wife, a devoted mother, a kind

---

neighbor and an earnest Christian. She was never very strong and the last few years quite frail; the last four months she was confined to the house and a part of the time to her bed and at times her sufferings were great, her disease being of the stomach."

"But her faith in God never faltered; her end was what might be expected from one who had served God so faithfully through life. She was free from suffering about two days before she died, and when the end came with her eyes Heavenward, she said, 'I see her,' then with one hand raised as though to greet someone she said, 'They are coming, praise God.' Then her pure gentle spirit took its departure to the home of the blest. 'Oh for the death of those, who slumber in the Lord: O be like theirs, my last repose like theirs, my last reward.'"

"Sister Glendenning leaves an aged father and mother who are in feeble health and nearing the 'crossing,' and a sorrowing husband, four children and one step-daughter who loved her as a mother and to whom she had been all that the name mother implies. The funeral sermon was preached by the writer from First Thessalonians 4:14, 'For if we believe that Jesus died and rose again, even so them also which sleep in Jesus will God bring with Him.'" S. A. Elliot.

New Family Arrives

When I was three years old (1896), mother married Peter Rush (stepfather).[23] He had a daughter, Fairy (stepsister),[24] one year and one week older than me. We grew up as sisters but were told different. Dad didn't adopt me; I kept my Glendenning name.

TWO DEATHS—ONE MARRIAGE

Sylvia's father, Robert Glendenning died in 1895 from a brain injury caused by a horse. That same year in Ringgold county, Peter Rush's wife, Estella (Pratt) died on August 5, about three months after Robert's death. Then less than one year after the two deaths, Peter Rush married Sylvia's mother, Mary Glendenning, in 1896. Sylvia was three years old when she gained a new step-sister, Fairy Rush. Sylvia's mother would go on to have seven children with Peter Rush—thus Sylvia gained two half-brothers and five half-sisters. Two deaths produced one marriage—how joy came out of sorrow.

---

[23] Peter's first wife, Sara (Ross), had two children with Peter. The oldest, John J. Glendenning, died before Sylvia was born, and Mary Olive Glendenning who married Curt Abarr. They had two children, Lela and Merele. Mary Olive died in in 1901 at the age of 39. Sylvia visited her gravesite in Montana in 1913.
[24] Fairy Belle Rush was born on October 24, 1892, nearly one year before Sylvia was born. Although Fairy was Sylvia's stepsister, Sylvia considered Fairy her sister. Fairy died on February 2, 1935. Fairy married Conrad Lawrence (born May 26, 1892; died April 19, 1967).

First Memories

The first I remember about my early life was when I was five. I remember being on the train headed for Montana. Grandpa Peter Glendenning had moved to Montana (1897) after my mother remarried. The folks (Peter and Rush) moved (1898) to Montana to Columbia Falls—not too far from Kalispell (photo below 1900).[25]

Peter Glendenning lived on a farm not too far away. Aunt Ollie and Uncle Curt Abarr lived out there too. Lela Abarr and I went to the timber with Grandpa, and he made each of us a little rolling pin out of wood. Fairy and I started to school. I remember I was told the first day of school to not come to school because I was too young. I was disappointed; Fairy and I had always been able to go together and do the same things. We only lived in Montana six months because the folks didn't like it out there.

Black Measles

The folks had a baby boy (Orville) before we went to Montana. While we were living in the first house we moved in after coming back, the baby and I had the Black Measles[26] that summer (1899). Dad's nephew came from Oklahoma

---

[25] Picture courtesy of Dale Jones.
[26] Black Measles is a darkened hemorrhagic cutaneous spots seen in Rocky Mountain spotted fever.

and came down with them also. Fairy was at her Grandma Pratt's[27] when we were exposed, so she didn't get them. My hair came out so badly that they cut my curls all off.

Sometime after this, Orville died; he was 2 years old.

Orville Rush

Orville Rush: Middle Fork Cemetery[28]

---

[27] Grandma Pratt was the mother of Peter Rush's first wife, Esther Pratt.
[28] "The stone in Middle Fork Cemetery has the wrong dates. It shows he was born September 25, 1895 and died September 14, 1897, but this should be born September 25, 1897 and died September 14, 1899. Mother said Grandmother Rush said they knew the dates were wrong but just never got around to having it corrected" (written by Robert Lay 3/31/1987).

Maps of the Farms

Robert Lay, Sylvia's oldest son, drew this map (photo below) of the key places where Sylvia lived while in Ringgold County. The map was made on February 3, 1971. It includes Sylvia's birthplace (Steadman farm), and Sylvia's grandparents' farms—Peter Glendenning and John Steadman.

By using this map along with farm maps of Ringgold County from 1894, 1915, and 1930, all of the farms Sylvia mentioned in her story and every school and church referred to, were located, identified, and photographed for this book during a three-year period, including five trips to Ringgold County.

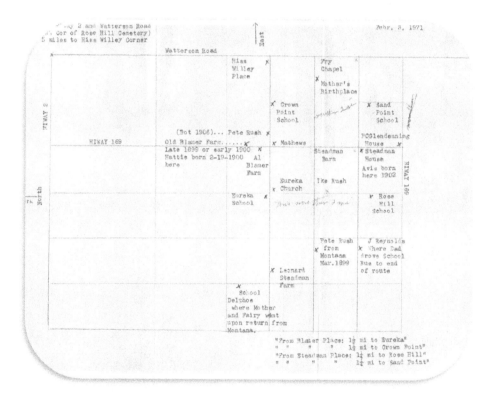

At the top of the map is east; west is on the bottom. North is on the left and south is on the right.

In the spirit of Robert's map-making work, a new map was produced by Douglas Lay, by hand, locating every farm, every school, every church where Sylvia either had lived or had attended. The overall map is included on the next pages.

SYLVIA'S LIFE IN RINGGOLD COUNTY   1893 TO 1935

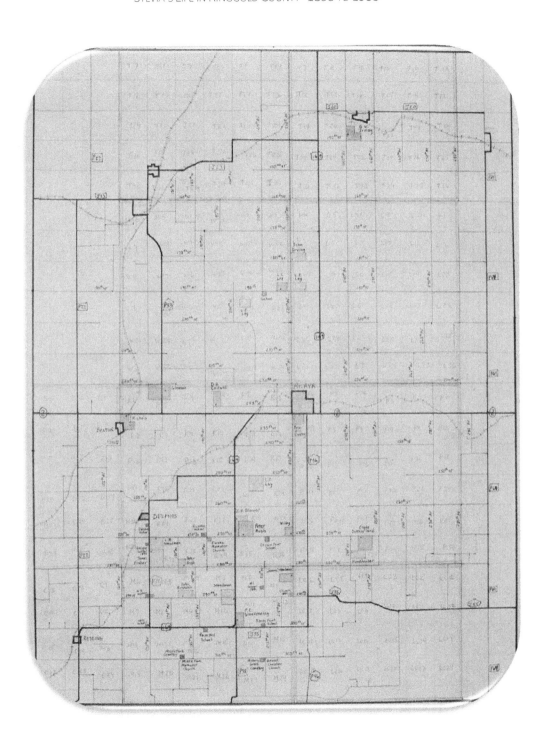

RICE AND MIDDLE FORK TOWNSHIPS

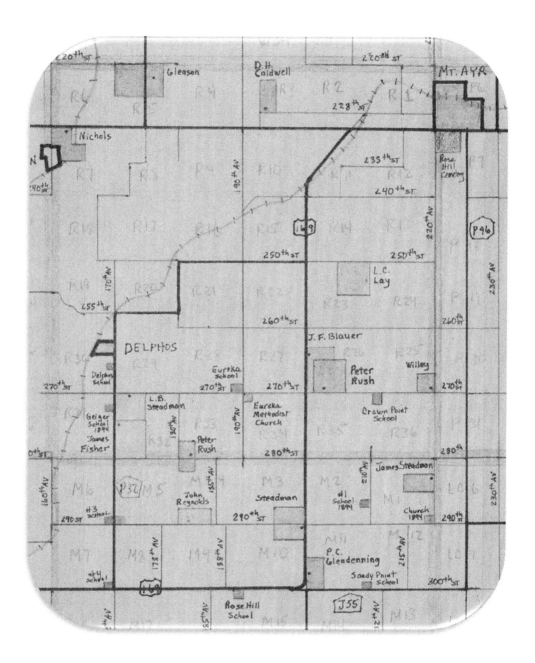

3

CITY OF "SISTERS"

1899-1902

At the age of five, Sylvia's new family would leave Montana after only six months and return to Ringgold County to settle down on a farm owned by the Rush family, southeast of Delphos. She would remain in Ringgold County for the next 36 years.

During this transition period, Sylvia would not only begin to put down roots in Iowa, but she would begin to build a close relationship with her new stepsister, Fairy, only about a year apart in age. They would forge a strong bond of love for each other. They would learn about honesty while picking up apples on the Fisher farm; they would be responsible for the care of Sylvia's new half-sister while the parents were working out in the fields; they would be surprised by their father while walking home from school; and they would share not only the good times but the consequences of a shared illness.

No Place Like Home

So we moved back to Iowa (March 1, 1899) in a small house (photo below: the Peter Rush family farm[29]) southeast of Delphos. We were in the Delphos school district.

CITY OF DELPHOS

The town, originally called Borneo, was changed in November of 1880 to Delphos, meaning "brother." The town was located on the C. B. and Q Railroad (photo next page)[30] between Mt. Ayr and Redding with four trains passing through town each day. The crew of the arriving freight train at noon, "would telegraph ahead, alerting the boarding house in Delphos as to how many would be ordering lunch that day. The station agent would relay the information to the boarding house. By the time the freight train arrived in Delphos and stopped on the main tracks, their lunch would be waiting for them at the boarding house."[31]

---

[29] The Peter Rush farm was in the Rice Township #33, corner of 280th St. and 180th Ave. (See *Ringgold County 1915 Ogle Iowa Historical Atlas* J.R. Rush).

[30] Photo courtesy of *digital.lib.uiowa.edu/raihaodinan*.

[31] http://iagenweb.org/ringgold/history/delphos/hist-delphos.html.

Train service, however, was discontinued in 1945 after 65 years of service, and the tracks were eventually removed. Large stockyards along with several businesses were present: a blacksmith, merchants, an elevator, a wagon shop, a hotel and a lumberyard, all by 1900. The first telephone was installed in 1896 (photo below: the Delphos Train Station[32]).

Sylvia Glendenning's grandfather, J. S. Stedman, was one of the first merchants in town around 1900, and Sylvia's aunt, Fannie F. Stedman, was one of the first postmasters. Later postmasters were Sylvia's Uncle, Ed Geiger, married to Hattie Steadman, and Eva Rice, Sylvia's aunt, married to Sim C. Rice (photo below: Delphos, 2014).

_____

[32] Photo courtesy of IAGenWeb.org/Ringgold County.

City of Delphos: Looking East (2014)

The First Baptist church (photo below) was built in 1883 with services twice a week. The original church was moved to Delphos in 1884 from its original location 3.5 miles northwest of Delphos. A second building was built in 1921, after the original building was torn down.

Sylvia's uncle, Benjamin F. Seaton, was part of the building committee for the new building. Sylvia's aunt, Fannie Steadman, was a member of the church in the late 1890's and sang in the choir. It is currently standing as of 2015.

The Christian Church was built a few years after the Baptist church in the late 1880's.

Sylvia's aunt, Hattie (Steadman) sang in the choir in the late 1890's. Although it is no longer in use, the building remains today (photo below).

Delphos was known at the turn of the century as "one of the cleanest and most circumspect towns in Ringgold County."[33] The 1899 population, the year Sylvia's family moved there, was 128. The 2010 census has the population at 25.

One Bad Apple

Fairy and I walked to school, and we had to pass a large orchard with no buildings around which belonged to old Mr. Fisher. We picked apples off the

---

[33] http://iagenweb.org/ringgold/history/delphos/hist-delphos.html.

ground and ate some. Because there were so many apples on the ground, we filled our dinner pails and took some home to the folks. The folks, however, told us we were stealing the apples and never to do it again. We didn't know we were stealing. We were just getting some apples to eat. That is when we learned our first lesson in honesty. I have never forgotten that lesson and the copy we used to write in school, "Honesty is the best policy."

Mr. Fisher's Farm[34]

Sylvia lived just over the top of the hill on the dirt road (top right-hand corner). To walk to school in Delphos, she would cut across the farm diagonally from the top right-hand corner to the bottom left-hand corner. Mr. Fisher's farm was on the corner of 280th street and County Highway P32, just south of Sylvia's Uncle Leonard Steadman's farm in Rice Township #32.

House of Flies

Then we moved to another farm, called the old Blauer place (photo next page[35]) after September 1899. The old house was full of flies. We had to fight them night and day. It was here that Hattie (half-sister) was born on Feb. 19,

[34] Mr. Fisher was James Fisher, whose son, Orr Cleveland Fisher, became an artist and painted the mural, "Evening on the Farm", in 1942, located at the Forest City Post Office. (See *Ringgold County 1915 Ogle Iowa Historical Atlas*).
[35] The location of the Blauer Place was in the Rice Township #26, east of Highway 169 and north of 270th St. A section of the Blauer farm would later be purchased by Peter Rush when he purchased his farm in 1905. (See *Ringgold County 1894 Iowa Historical Atlas*).

1900. I remember mother putting Hattie in the high chair and telling Fairy and me to watch her and not to take her out of the chair while mother went to the field to help gather a load of corn.

Switch Backs

Fairy and I had to walk about a mile and a half to school in the Eureka school district. The schoolhouse was across the corner from the Methodist church.[36]

We would play on the way home. Dad kept telling us if we didn't come straight home, some time he would be hiding. So sure enough, when we

---

[36] The Eureka School was located in the lower left-hand corner behind the fence posts in the photo above. (See *Ringgold County 1894 Historic Map Works*).

played again, dad jumped out from behind the bushes. He had a switch, and he switched our legs every little while all the way home for almost a mile.

EUREKA SCHOOL DISTRICT, NO. 8[37]

This is the schoolhouse (photo below) Sylvia and Fairy attended in 1899, only two years after this picture was taken. Sylvia would have attended school with some of the children in the photograph. The school was about 1.25 miles directly west of the Peter Rush farm on the corner of 270th street and 190th avenue.

Eureka School No. 8[38]

The schoolhouse was built in 1897 for $500. It measured 26 feet by 27 feet and could seat up to 40 kids. During the school year of 1898, there were plans to build 15 new country schools throughout Ringgold County based on this structure. The schoolhouse was in the Rice Township on the corner of 270th street and 190th avenue (#28 Rice Township). The school was 2.5 miles southwest of Delphos, Iowa

Crown Point

The next term of school (1900), we went to Crown Point School (photo

---

[37] A *Modern Country Schoolhouse*. http://iagenweb.org/ringgold/schools/misc/sch-eurekaNO8.html.

[38] Mount Ayr Depot Museum "Twice-A-Weekly News" Mount Ayr, IA 1898. Used by permission.

below[39]), about the same distance as the previous school. Fairy got whooping cough on the last day of school; I got it from her, and then Hattie got it. She was only about 6 months old.

---

[39] Crown Point School (R36) was most likely located in front of the line of trees in the distance in Rice Township #36. It is south of 270th street and east of 220th avenue, two miles east of Eureka School No. 8. (See *Ringgold County 1894 Historic Map Works*).

4

GRANDPA MEMORIES

1902-1905

When Sylvia was nine, she moved, with her family, back to her grandparents Steadman's farm, the farm where Sylvia had lived after her father accidently died in 1895. Grandpa and grandma Steadman had purchased a store in Delphos, about five miles northwest of the farm. The next three years for Sylvia would appear to be a time filled with rich memories of life on the farm—attending two different schools, participating in the children's program at church, welcoming Sylvia's second half-sister into the world, playing in the cherry tree orchards with the honey bees, riding a runaway horse when the parents were not at home, and getting into mischief with her cousins on the farm (photo below: Grandpa Steadman's Farm).

Home at School and Church

We moved from the Blauer place to Grandpa Steadman's farm on March of 1902. They had bought a store and had moved to Delphos. We didn't take any fleas with us; mother was very careful. We now went to the Rose Hill School (photo below[40]).

Another year we went to Sandy Point School (photo below[41]) because Fairy's aunt (Anna Pratt) was the teacher.

---

[40] The Rose Hill School was located in Middle Fork Township #16, south of Highway 169 and just east of 185th Av. The school was located where the trees are. (See *Ringgold County 1894 Historic Map Works*).
[41] Sandy Point School was located in the Middle Fork Township #11 just east of Peter Glendenning's farm on 300th St. The school was to the left of the telephone pole near the group of trees. (See *Ringgold County 1894 Historic Map Works*).

We went to Hickory Grove to Sunday school, and we were in the children's day program. We rode to practice with the neighbors. We lived on their farm for three or four years—not sure.

HICKORY GROVE ADVENT CHRISTIAN CHURCH[42]

Sylvia's family attended the Advent Christian Church, built in 1888 and dedicated on January 13, 1889, located in the Middle Fork Township. The church got its name because of the hickory groves on the current property, owned by Mrs. Susan Brown, who held church meetings at her home. The church was three miles southeast of the Steadman's farm. The church held its last service on June 21, 2015, over a 126-year period. The church is still standing as of 2015.

Sylvia's uncle, Thomas Glendenning,[43] was a member of the church and later became an elder. When the church was between pastors, Thomas would fill the pulpit.

Thomas was married three times. His first wife, Emma (Gretta) died on November 18, 1893. She is buried in the Hickory Grove Cemetery. Thomas would marry again,

[42] *Hickory Grove Advent Church.* http://iagenweb.org/ringgold/church/files/ch-hickorygrove.html.
[43] Thomas Glendenning was the oldest brother of Robert Glendenning, Sylvia's father. Thomas was born on November 7, 1866 and died on November 16, 1938.

this time to Claudia (Hass), yet they were divorced in 1907, unusual not only for that time period, but also for a preacher. Thomas married a third time to Blanch (Dyer). She was born in 1892 and died in 1962. When Thomas died in 1938, he was buried next to his first wife, Emma

Thomas and Emma Glendenning

HICKORY GROVE CEMETERY

The Hickory Grove cemetery, located on the property of the Hickory Grove Advent Christian Church, was established in 1899 and is listed on the National Register of Historic Places. It is in the Middle Fork Township #23 on the corner of 210th Av. and

310th St.

Several members of John Lay's family are buried here: Homer and Anna Lay (John's brother and sister-in-law); their son, Wilbur Lay and his wife, Madelyn Lay; and the only daughter of Homer and Anna Lay, Blanche, who died at birth in 1918.

Hickory Grove Cemetery

Left to Right: Blanche Lay, Madelyn and Wilbur Lay, Anna and Homer Lay

Several members of Sylvia's family are buried here, including her grandparents, John and Delia Steadman and her uncle, Thomas Glendenning and his wife, Emma. Also,

Estrella (Pratt) Rush, the first wife of Sylvia's step-father, Peter Rush, is buried here.

Delia and John Stedman, Sylvia's Maternal Grandparents

Thomas and Emma Glendenning

Esther (Pratt) Rush

Second-Half Sister

While we lived there (J. S. Stedman's farm), Avis was born on December 16, 1902. Fairy and I found the baby clothes before Avis was born. We showed them to a neighbor girl, and she went home and told. Then Fairy storied, and she got a whipping. I guess in those days people were ashamed to let people know they were expecting a baby. If I wanted to go out to play, I would have to get Avis to sleep first. I would shake the cot she was on and tell her,

"If you don't shut your eyes, the dogs will get you."

Ester Addison (L) and Avis Rush (R)[44]

Traveling Salesman

When Fairy and I would get home from school, if the folks were gone, we were to start supper. One evening, I was frying potatoes for supper. A man

---

[44] Ester Addison was the daughter of Sylvia's aunt, Sarah Alice (Steadman) Addison.

came to the door selling fruit pictures. I told him the folks were gone, and I invited him to stay for supper. I was teased plenty about inviting him; however, he declined the invitation.

The Orchard

We had fun out in the big orchard. We had a big sweet cherry tree where we would climb in and eat the cherries. Grandpa Steadman also had a large number of beehives in the large orchard. When the honey was ready, he would come out and take the honey from the hives. Fairy and I would watch and eat honey.

Name Calling

On the way home from school (Sandy Point School) one afternoon, Fairy, Millie Hardin—a neighbor girl—and I called a mean boy a bad name. We didn't think he heard us because we were going across the field and he went around the road. Millie had two sisters with us, so we thought they tattled. Anyway, the next day the teacher whipped the three of us.

Runaway Ride

One day the folks went to the field to work. They told us to water the stock. The pasture was on one side of the road and the windmill and water tank were on the other side (photo below).

We decided we would ride across, so we both got on one horse without a bridle or halter, and we got on facing her tail. The horse went all right until she got in the middle of the road. She started bucking, and we both landed in the dirt. I tore my dress. We went to the house and tried to sew it up.

Teachers' Lessons

One year a teacher boarded with us. It was from her we learned to read in bed. We had never heard of such a thing. One day, two teachers (the one boarding with us and Anna Pratt) dressed up in men's clothes and went up the road to scare us. No one ever saw a woman dress that way, so they made us think they were old tramps. So we thought we would do the same thing; only we blacked our faces.

Driving Without a License

Once the folks decided to go to Guthrie County on a visit. They, along with Hattie and Avis (they were both small), and Mother's sister, Eva,[45] and brother, Leonard[46] drove dad's mules hitched to a wagon. I guess the trip could be made much quicker now. They got Clark Pratt[47] to do chores. Anna Pratt, who was teaching school east of us, stayed to keep the other teacher company who was boarding with us. We had a mare we called *Old Mae*. She was very gentle. We rode her to school in the winter if the weather was bad. We also knew how to harness and hitch her to the buggy. But this time, the folks said,

"Don't drive her while we are gone."

But Aunt Jessie Rush[48] called and said they had butchered, and if we came over, she would give us some fresh meat. So Fairy and I hitched up Old Mae to the buggy and started over after the meat. I was driving and thought I was

---

[45] Eva Gertrude Steadman was the fourth of six children by Sylvia's grandparents, James and Delia Steadman. Eva married Sim C. Rice.

[46] Leonard B. Steadman was the youngest of six children by Sylvia's grandparents, James and Delia Steadman. Leonard married Mae E. (Rice) and they had one son, Burt Steadman.

[47] Clark Pratt was the brother-in-law of Peter Rush, Sylvia's stepfather. Clark was the brother of Esther Estrella Rush, the first wife of Peter Rush.

[48] Aunt Jessie Rush was married to Isaac W. Rush, the brother of Peter Rush, Sylvia's stepfather. Jessie was born in 1876 and died May 30, 1934. Isaac Rush was born on June 6, 1872 and died on July 18, 1944.

getting too close to a little ditch, so I pulled over in the road. Our buggy wheel and Allen Clewel's[49] wheel caught together, and I broke our buggy. Fairy and I left the buggy, got on the horse, and went on horseback to get the meat. Dad had to get the buggy after he got home from Guthrie County (photo below: similar type of buggy used by Sylvia)[50].

The Shot Heard Around the Farm

One day, Ona and Alta Rush[51] had been visiting at Olive's[52] house and came on to our house to stay all night. While there, Howard[53] shot at a tin can on the water pump and hit Ona in the hip. She told us kids, but she didn't want the folks to know. Mother put us to churning in a fruit jar. We were all taking turns, shaking, but Ona's hip hurt. I guess the shaking didn't do it any good. We persuaded her to tell mother. She did, and the folks called her dad to go home and go to the doctor.

---

[49] Allen Clewell was a neighbor of Sylvia's parents, Peter and Mary Rush. Allen was born in 1875 and died in 1947.
[50] Picture public domain.
[51] Ona and Alta Rush were Sylvia's cousins and the children of Isaac and Jessie (Johnson) Rush. Isaac Rush was the brother of Peter Rush, Sylvia's stepfather. Ona married Mr. Miller and Alta married Mr. Tillotson.
[52] Olive Rush was a cousin of Sylvia Lay and the daughter of Siretus and Margaret (Anderson) Rush. Sirestus was a brother of Peter Rush. Olive Rush married Thomas Bellew. Olive was born on May 5, 1890 and died May 25, 1987. Thomas Bellew was born in 1892 and died in 1973. Olive's brother was Howard Rush.
[53] Howard Rush was a cousin of Sylvia Lay and the son of Sirestus and Margaret (Anderson) Rush. Howard Rush married Stellia (DeFenbaugh). Howard was born on January 28, 1894 and died in 1957.

The Churning

One day Mother told Fairy and I to churn with a barrel churn. We were to turn it round and round with a crank or handle. We opened the lid to see if it was done, but we forgot to fasten the lid again. When we turned it, the cream landed on the floor. We scooped it up and finished churning. When mother came in from the field, she salted the butter and saw specks in it. She started to pick them out, and then it dawned on her what had happened. She had to throw the butter away. Fairy, however, had told her we spilled the dishwater and made the spot on the wood floor. So as usual, Dad gave her a whipping.

Mother's Milk

One time the folks went to help care for Grandpa Pratt. Olive came to stay with us. One cow wouldn't let anyone but mother milk her, so Olive put on mother's dress and bonnet and milked the cow.

GRANDPA PRATT

Grandpa Pratt, known as Levi Clark Pratt, was the father of Esther Pratt, Sylvia's step-father's, (Peter Rush), first wife. Levi became sick in November of 1905 and Sylvia's mother and step-father would help to take care of Levi. This is her reference from above. Later in 1906, Levi would pass away. His obituary is listed below. [54]

"Levi Clark Pratt was born October 13, 1837, at Craftsbury, Vermont. His father and mother both died before he was two years of age. He was married March 12, 1865, to Sarah Goodall in Morgan County, Ill. To this union were born seven children - five daughters and two sons. Six children survive him, one daughter, Mrs. Peter RUSH, having died August 5, 1895. He was stricken down November 20, 1905, and although suffering intensely night and day he bore it patiently until the end, which came Sunday morning, August 19, 1906. He was at the time of his death aged 68 years, 10 months, and six days."

"He united with the A. C. church about 16 years ago, and was a consistent member of the same at the time of his death. He was deeply interested in the Lord's work. The last time he was away from his home he was at a service in this house. Not long ago I talked with Brother PRATT concerning the work here and he said he hoped the brethren would not allow Christian work here to die out."

---

[54] Mount Ayr Record News.

"He was conscious until almost the hour of death, and although life was sweet he did not fear death. In the death of Brother PRATT the community has lost a good and useful citizen, his wife has lost a kind and loving husband and the children a tender and affectionate father. To the family I would say serve God faithfully that you may be reunited on the resurrection morn in the kingdom of God."

LEVI CLARK PRATT FAMILY[55]

Front Row (L to R)
Mary Jane (1876-1917); William Levi (1884-1962); Sarah (Goodall) (1844-1934)
Back row (L to R)
Anna Elizabeth (Lay) (1879-1969); Etta Leonora (1869-1931); Levi Clark (1837-1906);
Clark Mills (1880-1942); Clara Belle (1866-1966)

SARAH PRATT

The wife of Levi Pratt, Sarah, was the mother of Sylvia's step-father's first wife. After her husband, Levi, died in 1906, she continued to live on the family farm in Lotts Creek Township until 1919 when she moved to Mt. Ayr. It is most likely that Sylvia's mother and step-father continued to help take care of her during this time. Sarah died in 1934 and her obituary is listed below.[56]

---

[55] The picture is courtesy of Ringgold Co. IA GenWeb.org/Ringgold County. This picture was taken after the death of the third daughter, Esther Estella.
[56] Mount Ayr Record-News.

"Sarah PRATT was born November 30, 1844 [Morgan Co. IL], and died July 23, 1934, aged 89 years, seven months, and 23 days. Sarah GOODALL, the daughter of William and Jane (HODGSON) GOODALL, was born on a farm near Jacksonville, Morgan County, Illinois. She spent her childhood and youth on the old farm there, and when she was 21 (sic) years old was married to Levi C[lark] PRATT on March 12, 1865 [Morgan Co. IL]. To this union seven children were born, namely: Clara, Etta, Estella, Mary Ann (sic, should be Mary, Anna), Clark and William."

"In the spring of 1880 she, with her husband and five daughters, came in a covered wagon to Ringgold County, Iowa, and established their pioneer home on the prairie land of Middle Fork Township. Later they moved to a farm in Lotts Creek Township. At this place her husband died on August 19, 1906. In 1919 she moved to Mount Ayr, where she lived until her health so failed that she was unable to keep house longer, and four and one-half years ago she came to live with her daughter, Mrs. Anna LAY, where she made her home until her death."

"Her family circle was first broken by the death of Mrs. Estella RUSH, who died on August 5, 1895. This was followed by the death of her husband in 1906. On March 27, 1917, Mrs. Mary PATCH died. On January 6, 1931, the family circle was broken once more by the death of another daughter, Mrs. Etta PATCH."

"About forty-five years ago Mrs. PRATT was converted and baptized by Elder F. C. WATKINS and united with the Hickory Grove Advent Christian Church, and remained a truly consecrated Christian until she fell asleep in Jesus on Monday evening about six o'clock. She had a gentle, kind disposition, and was always cheerful and uncomplaining. She was a loving, self-sacrificing mother and a friend to all she came in contact with. She greatly enjoyed attending church and Sunday school and went as long as her health permitted."

"Among those who are left to mourn are Mrs. Clara STRAWN of Vista, California, Mrs. Anna LAY of Mount Ayr, Clark PRATT of Benton, William PRATT of Oakes, N. D. There are also 30 grandchildren and 33 great-grandchildren; two brothers, Thomas GOODALL of Shenandoah and James GOODALL of Kentucky, who are the only ones left of a family of eleven children."

5

Let the Angels Rejoice

1905-1908

As Sylvia entered into her early teen years, she would be moving again, this time off of her grandparent's farm and on to a farm purchased by her stepfather (photo below). She would call this home until she was married in 1914. The move also meant she started to attend a different church and a different school again, this time outside of Delphos. Sylvia's family would continue to grow as she welcomed three more half-sisters and a half-brother. Sylvia would still spend time with her grandparents and her Aunt Mae and Uncle Leonard Steadman.

Peter Rush's Farm

Dad bought a farm and made a schoolhouse into a house.[57] When I was about twelve, we moved there and lived there until I was married on February 11, 1914. Louise, Lucille, Delia, and Arthur were born to the folks in this house on this farm. Uncle Leonard had moved on Grandpa's farm when we moved off.

SYLVIA'S FAMILY AROUND 1921

Back Row:
Avis (Helzell), Fairy (Lawrence), Hattie (Jackson), Louise (Peckman)
Middle Row:
Sylvia (Lay), Mary Ollie (Steadman) Rush, Peter Rush, Lucille (Harrison)
Front Row:
Delia (Baser), Arthur Rush

---

[57] The Peter Rush farm was in the Rice Township #26, north of 270th St. and about ¼ mile east of Highway 169. Peter purchased part of the Blauer farm where Sylvia had lived previously. (See *Ringgold County 1915 Ogle Iowa Historical Atlas*).

Our Happiest Time

We had to change schools again. This time I went to Crown Point where I finished 8th grade. Before we went to school at Crown Point, we had to wash the dishes and get the cows milked before we went. Louise was born the first spring we were there. While mother was in bed, Fairy and I made the garden and did all the housework. We had a big hammock in the front yard and dad made us a croquet ground. As we grew a little older, we started going to parties in the winter. That was our happiest time.

Let the Angels Rejoice

We went to Sunday school and Church at Eureka. We could walk. Fairy and I joined the church and were baptized at a pond near the church. She was sprinkled, but I believed in immersion, so I went under the water. I had to ride home in wet clothes. Mother couldn't be there because she was pregnant with Lucille, and pregnant women didn't appear in public.

Sylvia was most likely baptized across from the church in the pond in the distance. The church was in the Rice Township (#34) on the corner of 270th street and 190th avenue. The view is from 270th street, looking southwest. The Rev. Arthur Eastman was the minister during this time.

Home Away From Home

I spent quite a bit of time at Grandma Steadman's. I felt like Grandma's was my house. She said I was more like a daughter than a granddaughter. One year I stayed there and went to school (photo below) in a house on the edge of Delphos.[58] In later years, Uncle Curt Willey lived there, grandma's brother. Aunt Eva and Uncle Leonard were still in school. They went in the schoolhouse. Later Delphos had a two-room schoolhouse outside Delphos.

I sat with Ona Rush at school, so I could study with her out of her books. Dad wouldn't get Fairy and me our own books, so we had to share them and study together. We had one tablet between us. One time she got the book with the picture, and the next time I got it.

The Sound of Music

Two summers I stayed at Grandpa's and took piano lessons from Mrs.

---

[58] The one-room schoolhouse was just south of the line of trees in the distance. The two-room schoolhouse was to the left of the Delphos sign on the top of the hill on County Highway P32. The view is looking north. Sylvia would later teach at the two-room schoolhouse in the fall of 1910. (See *Ringgold County 1894 Iowa Historical Atlas*).

Whitlatch,[59] a music teacher in Delphos. We had an organ at home. When I took music lessons on the organ, Ollie Rush was my teacher. One summer I stayed and took treatment from an osteopath lady doctor who came down to Delphos on the train from Mt. Ayr.

Baby Sitting

One spring Aunt Mae[60] wanted me to stay with them and help with Burt Steadman who was a baby still in his baby buggy. I went to school during the day and watched him in the evening. Because she said she would buy my clothes, she got me all fixed up with clothes.

Burt Steadman (L) and
Louise Rush (R)

---

[59] Mrs. Whitlatch and her husband, Owen, lived in Delphos on South Street at the west end of town.
[60] Aunt Mae Steadman was married to Leonard Steadman, Sylvia's uncle and the brother of Sylvia's mother, Mary Ollie. Aunt Mae had a son, Burt.

Nell for Christmas

I was at Aunt Mae's about two months when mother came and said dad said I had to come home to help with the work as mother was pregnant again. So I went back home.

Aunt Mae and Uncle Leonard's Farm[61]

That winter, Nell was born on December 15th. Dad decided he wanted goose for Christmas dinner, so he invited company for dinner, yet mother was still in bed. We girls did the work when Nell was born as well as when Louise was born. Aunt Emma Elliott[62] took pity on us. She always seemed to take our part and came over and dressed the goose.

All Work and No Play

One Thanksgiving, all the girls in the neighborhood were invited to the Clayton's for dinner, but Fairy and I were not through shucking corn. We pleaded with dad to let us go to the dinner, but he said we had to work. We

---

[61] The farm was south of 270th street and east of County Highway P32, half a mile south of Delphos in the Rice Township #32. (See *Ringgold County 1915 Ogle Iowa Historical Atlas*).
[62] Aunt Emma Elliott was the sister of Peter Rush. Emma married Allamando Elliott. Emma was born on November 17, 1868 and died on August 1, 1963. Allamando was born in 1865 and died in 1946.

told him we would miss school on Monday to help finish the corn, but he wouldn't let us go. So we went to the field and got one load of corn, but then it started to rain. Even though we couldn't work, it was too late to go to the Claytons. Again, Aunt Emma Elliott came to our rescue. Although her daughter had gone to the dinner, Aunt Emma invited us to her house, and she made cherry pie—my favorite. But that evening we just sat there, knowing the other girls at the Clayton's were having fun.

Preparation for Ministry

The year Avis started to school, we had a male teacher—John Areal. He taught us Bible verses. I guess he couldn't do that now; he would be penalized. One day this teacher was standing at the top of a very slick hill which we would go coasting down. He had a hand in each pocket. So Fairy and Olive slipped up behind him and pushed his feet out from under him. He fell and tore his coat pockets but didn't say a word. In later years, he became a minister in Boston.

SYLVIA LAY'S
HALF-SISTERS
(1906 OR 1907)

(L to R) Avis, Louise,
Hattie

Revival in the Land

We attended Sunday school and church at Eureka, a country church. We walked 1.5 miles to Sunday school on Sunday, and when revival meetings were in progress, we walked in warm weather. In the winter, some neighbors would pick everyone up along the way in a bobsled. The folks went to the preaching service but didn't go to Sunday school. One time mother unwrapped the baby in church, but she had forgotten to pull the dirty clothes off her feet. Later Fairy and I became members of the church. In later years, the church was closed, and now it isn't there anymore. The memberships were moved to Mt. Ayr Methodist Church (photo below).[63]

Vacation with Grandparents

One winter Grandpa and Grandma Steadman went to California. They sent back a crate of lemons and oranges. Another winter they went to Florida, and one time they went to Ohio to visit Grandpa's brother. When Grandpa got

---

[63] This current building, constructed in 1912, replaced an older building at the current site. The building is at the corner of Madison and Pierce Streets. Bishop Joseph Berry officiated at the dedication of the new facility on April 28, 1912. It was built at a cost of over $26,000. (IaGenWeb.org/Ringgold County).

off the train at one station to stretch his legs, he got on the train going in the direction he had come from. Grandma thought he was in the smoking car. After the train had travelled a while, the conductor came and asked if she was Mrs. Steadman. But Grandpa had the tickets and all the money in his pocket, so he had to wire Grandma to get off the train at the next station and wait for him.

Food and Fun

The first time I went to town on Memorial Day, Fairy and I went with Ollie and Howard Rush. They drove a horse and buggy. We took our lunch and ate in the buggy. Mother didn't allow me to go with boys until I was 16. I was always invited to the parties, so Fairy always took me with her and her boyfriend. Hattie was just a kid but she and some her age found some cigars and smoked one. She sure was sick. Fairy and I were invited to her Aunt Anna's wedding, and I never dreamed then she would someday by my sister-in-law.

MY SISTER IS MY AUNT

Aunt Anna was the sister of Peter Rush's first wife, Esther (Pratt). After Esther died in 1895, Peter Rush married Sylvia's mother, Mary Steadman in 1897, after her husband, Robert Glendenning died. Peter Rush became Sylvia's step-father, and Anna became Sylvia's step-aunt. Then 12 years later, Anna Pratt married Homer Lay on February 26, 1908. Six years later, Sylvia married John Lay, the brother of Homer. Consequently, Sylvia's aunt Anna became also Sylvia's sister-in-law! (photo right: Wedding Picture of Homer and Anna Lay, Feb. 26, 1908).

6

From Student to Teacher

1908-1913

The next five years would find Sylvia moving from childhood to young adulthood as she replaces her student's books for a teacher's desk. She would finish high school early, study and receive her teacher's certificate, begin teaching in a two-room schoolhouse where she once attended as a child, and then prepare for the greatest change of her life with the arrival of a new family in town—the Lay family.

School House North of Mt Ayr (2014)

High Cost of Education

When I finished the 8th grade, (Spring 1909) I decided I wanted to go to High School. I had to pay tuition to go to High School then and pay for my board and room and most of my clothes. I asked mother, and she said I could go if I would use my own money. I had inherited a few dollars from a distant relative of Grandmother Glendenning named Hollingsworth. It came a little at a time as a lawsuit was in progress.

MT. AYR HIGH SCHOOL (1895-1912)[64]

Sylvia graduated from this school in 1911, the second to last graduating class in this building. Mount Ayr's second brick High School (photo below) was built in 1895. Because this schoolhouse did not have a gymnasium, basketball games were played at the Opera House in Mount Ayr. The Class of 1912 was the last class to graduate from this school that was torn down to make way for a larger and more modern school.

Bashful Days

When I started to high school (fall 1909) I was so bashful it was pitiful. I rode

[64] Picture courtesy of IAGenWeb.org/Ringgold County.

to school in Mt. Ayr with Reece Elliott for a while, and then I stayed in town. I boarded with Mrs. Dr. Poment[65] for a while. Then grandma Steadman told me of a girl, an old maid, who wanted a roommate, so I moved in with Mae Granger. She probably wasn't so old, but it seemed that way to me at that time. It was cheaper since I could bring food from home. We rented two rooms from Mrs. Webb.[66] We had a bed in the kitchen, so we had a living room without a bed. Neither one of us had boyfriends, so we did no entertaining (photo right: the original site of the 1915 high school).

Spooky Pneumonia

In my first year of high school, I had pneumonia. Mother came in town and cared for me in February. Before I was strong enough to go back to school, Aunt Jeda,[67] Olive's mother, asked me to stay there a while, so I spent some time there. While there, Ollie, Howard, and I decided to explore a big house that was empty. It was so big and so many rooms. It was spooky and one could almost get lost in it. When I was able to go back to school, I went back to our apartment. I went home on weekends.

---

[65] I was unable to identify Mrs. Dr. Poment.

[66] I was unable to identify Mrs. Webb.

[67] Aunt Jeda was Margaret Geneva (Anderson), but Sylvia referred to her as Jeda. She was born December 3, 1866 and died October 17, 1942. Aunt Jeda married Sirestus M. Rush, a brother of Sylvia's stepfather, Peter Rush. They had three children: Friend Rush, Olive Rush, and Howard Rush.

A John Letter

A new family had moved in our community that winter. I met them at Sunday school—the Lay family. All the young people sang in the choir. We met on Sunday evening to practice. In April, we met at Ed Blauer's. I was to ride back to town with aunt Jeda. John Lay wanted to take me to town but was too bashful to ask me, so Roy Blauer asked me to go with John. He had to coax a while then I said I would go; I went with him for almost three years.

LUTHER AND JANE LAY AND FAMILY[68]

L to R: Luther Lay, Luella Lay, John J. Lay (sitting); Sarah Jane (Irving); Veda Lay; Joseph Lay (Sitting); Homer Lay; Abner Lay

No Financial Aid

I stayed at home during the summer after my second year of high school and helped mother because she was pregnant with Delia. Dad said if I would stay and help he would buy my clothes. He paid for material for a dress that cost 12 cents per yard, and I bought a coat and charged it to myself. However, I discovered my dad had not paid my doctor's bill when I had pneumonia. The doctor told me that Dad said to wait until I could pay it myself.

Graduation Early

I quit high school during my second year (1911). That summer, I took the

---

[68] Picture courtesy of IAGenWeb.org/Ringgold County.

teacher's exam and passed. At that time, a High School diploma wasn't required to teach in rural schools. That fall, Elsie Hollaway Moffett[69] came over and asked me to apply to the Delphos School. She was teaching 5th through 8th grade. They needed a teacher for the first four grades. I was still so timid and afraid I would be turned down. Elsie took me over, and we sat on the steps of the Baptist Church (photo right) getting up the courage before asking for the job.

Mr. Morg Evans[70], the director, said I could have the teaching job, but I would have to put the fire out in the heater every evening and start a fresh fire every morning as the stove wasn't safe to keep a fire in overnight. Elsie and I would stay after school to sweep and clean up.

One evening, the big boys on their way home from school set a pasture on fire. The blaze came toward the schoolhouse. When we saw it, it was almost to the house. We ran out with our brooms and started fighting the fire, but some of the men in the neighborhood had seen it and came and put out the fire.

Another time, one of the fourth graders, who was larger than me, disobeyed me. I sent the little boys after a switch. Because he said I could not whip him, Elsie said she would help. I said no; I would do it. So we locked the door, Elsie took the key and went in her room, and I switched him.

---

[69] I was unable to identify Elsie Hollaway Moffett.
[70] Morg Evans owned a store that later was converted to a house of Henry Cavender.

Two-Room Delphos School[71]

LIFE OF A COUNTRY SCHOOL HOUSE TEACHER[72]

When Sylvia began teaching in the fall of 1911, she was expected to follow a set of strict rules common for public school teachers at the turn of the 20th century. Listed below are rules from an actual 1905 teaching contract for Story County, Iowa.

"Teachers are expected to live in the community in which they are employed and to take residence with local citizens for room and board. (Many teachers lived with the students and their parents going from one house to another)."

"It is understood that teachers will attend church each Sunday and take an active part, particularly in choir and Sunday school work."

"Dancing, card playing and the theatre are works of the Devil that lead to gambling, immoral climate, and influence and will not be tolerated."

"When laundering petticoats and unmentionables it is best to dry them in a flour sack or pillow case. (So no one sees them hanging on the line to dry)."

"Any teacher who smokes cigarettes, uses liquor in any form, frequents a pool or public hall, or (for men) gets shaved in a barber shop, (or for women) bobbs (cuts) her hair, has dyed hair, wears short skirts (could not be any shorter than 2 inches

---

[71] The view is looking south to the Delphos School from the front steps of the Baptist Church. The two-room school house was in the distance in the middle of the picture.
[72] Courtesy of Amehistory.org.

above the ankles) and has undue use of cosmetics will not be tolerated under any circumstances."

"Teachers will not marry or keep company with a man friend during the week except as an escort to church services. (The only man a woman teacher could be seen with was her father or her brother)."

A Teacher's Certificate from 1895.[73]

"Loitering in ice cream parlors, drug stores, etc., is prohibited."

"Purchasing or reading the Sunday Supplement on the Sabbath will not be tolerated."

"Discussing political views or party choice is not advisable."

"After 10 hours in school, the teacher should spend the remaining time reading the Bible or other good books."

"Women teachers who marry or engage in other unseemly conduct will be

---

[73] Rod Library, University of Northern Iowa. Teaching certificate from Adams County, Iowa, August 24, 1895.

dismissed."

"Every teacher should lay aside from his pay a goodly sum for his declining years so that he will not become a burden on society."

"The teacher who performs his labors faithfully and without fault for five years will be given an increase of 25 cents a week in his pay providing the Board of Education approves."

Staying at the Store

Grandma said I could board with them while I taught. She and Aunt Eva would not take any pay. Aunt Eva and Uncle Sim Rice[74] had bought half interest in Grandpa's store in Delphos so they moved in with Grandpa and Grandma. Uncle Leonard had married and moved on Grandpa's farm when the folks moved off.

Sylvia's grandfather, James Steadman, purchased the Baker store around 1900,[75]

Grandma always managed to see I fixed plenty for lunch. If I wouldn't, she would go to the store and get fruit. In those days, what was in the store

---

[74] Aunt Eva was the sister of Sylvia's mother, Mary Ollie Steadman. She was married to Sim C. Rice.
[75] Courtesy of IAGenWeb.org/Ringgold County.

belonged to the owner; he didn't have to give an account to the government or pay taxes like now. When Grandma needed anything from the store, she just took it off the shelf and took it home—simple as that.

Bible Battle

I went home on the weekends. John (photo below) would take me back to Grandma's on Sunday evening. One night he had stayed late, and we heard Grandpa get up. Because he had the reputation of having always run off his daughters', John grabbed his hat, got to the door, but then reconsidered. He sat down. Grandpa came downstairs, went to the kitchen, got an onion, and ate some because he said he had a cough. John knew he loved to talk Bible, so he asked Grandpa a question about that morning's Sunday school lesson. Grandpa explained it, talked Bible for a while and then went back upstairs to bed. He never said a word about my being up late.

Waiting for his Bride

When I arrived in Diagonal on my way home from Montana (Sylvia's visit to see her grandpa Glendenning, Chapter 1), it was night and a terrible storm—lighting, thunder, and pouring down rain—had closed the train station. But John had come to meet me; he was standing in the rain, waiting when I got off the train. It was nearly morning when I got home and into bed. Mother let me sleep till the evening, and then she came in and said,

> "I hate to wake you, but I want you to stay with the baby while I go plant some seed."

Fun before Work

That summer (1913) I went to summer school and stayed with Aunt Jeda.[76] Olive and I had fun. We had water fights with the boys. Cass Main owned the house and boarded with them, and Aunt Jeda's father lived with them. One night when Uncle Ras and Aunt Jeda were gone, Olive and I went upstairs to go to bed—we had limburger cheese on the head of the bed and on the door knob! Cass Main and Olive's brothers (Friend and Howard Rush) had played a joke on us. Then they came up in the hall. I guess they wanted to keep us in the smelly room. We were all making so much noise. I can still hear Olive's Grandpa, at the stair door, yell,

> "What in the hell is going on up there?"

Off to Work I Go

That fall (1913) I taught at the Rose Hill School. The school was divided into fall term, winter term, and spring term. I taught beginners through the 8th grade during the fall term. Uncle Dave Glendenning was the director.

Teacher's pay wasn't much so to save board money meant quite a bit. My pay was forty-two dollars a month. At the end of the month, I had to drive several miles to get my check. Dad said I could have a horse to drive if I wanted to

---

[76] Aunt Jeda was Margaret Geneve (Anderson) Rush, married to Sirestus Marion Rush, the brother of Peter Rush, Sylvia's stepfather. They had three children: Friend Rush, Olive Rush, and Howard Rush.

stay at home, so I drove back and forth every day. It was close to 4 miles. Percy Rush[77], one of the pupils, had been hurt, so his mother (Aunt Jessie) said if I would stop and let him ride to school when the weather was bad, I could stay there and she would board the horse and me. So if it was very rainy, I stayed there. They lived a little over a mile from school. This was the same school I had attended when I was small. Two little girl beginners I had were daughters of one of the old teachers, Fanny Savilie.

Uncle Dave asked if I wanted to teach the next year (1914). I turned him down and stayed home and did some sewing and made quilts, comforters, and got rugs ready for a rag carpet for the bedroom. I only signed for the fall term (1913) as John and I were planning on getting married that winter.

---

[77] Percy Rush was one of nine children of Isaac Rush (Peter Rush's brother) and Jessie May (Johnson).

7

Wedding Bells

1914

Snow began to fall at noon during the winter of 1914 as Sylvia Glendenning gave her vows to become the wife of John L. Lay (photo right) at the home of Sylvia's stepfather, Peter Rush, Unlike today, Sylvia did not have a wedding planner, a cook to cater the reception dinner, or a photographer to remember the special day. Rather, several days before the wedding, Sylvia began the preparations — baking numerous types of cakes for the reception, cooking and preparing the food, cleaning the house and arranging the rooms for the service. The service was well attended and was written up in the local paper in Mt. Ayr.

Wedding Day

We were married February 11, 1914 on Uncle Leonard and Aunt Mae's wedding day. We were married at my parent's home by Rev. Arthur Eastman. Aunt Mae made my wedding dress and mother made what was then called the second-day dress. I wanted to be married on Grandpa and Grandma's anniversary, (Feb. 6, 1823) but it wasn't on the day of the week we wanted (photo below: Sylvia and John Lay's Wedding).

The Wedding Planner

We invited 85 guests for dinner. Mother got a big meal—everything you could mention. For dessert, she had fruit salad and at least four kinds of cakes and several kinds of pies. Mother and I had expected to start baking cakes on Monday before the wedding on Wednesday, but Sunday night Friend Rush[78] came for mother because their baby was due to arrive.

The next morning, Monday, Aunt Emma came to the rescue again. She called and wanted to know if she could help me. I told her yes, so she came and we made cakes all day—white, black, burnt, sugar. Grandma Steadman made two beautiful angel food cakes—one for each table.

Mother got home, and Tuesday we dressed fourteen old hens; we roasted ten and creamed four. Some job! Aunt Eva came and fixed up the front room by putting up lace curtains back of where we were to stand.

Day of the Wedding

On Wednesday morning, the day of our wedding, we got up very early and took down every bed in the house. We carried four beds and bedding out to the washhouse and swept and cleaned the bedrooms. Mother put a long table in the room and one in the kitchen. About noon it started to snow. We had a hard snow all day. Then that evening we carried all the beds through the snow into the house and made the beds.

THE WEDDING OF JOHN LAY AND SYLVIA GLENDENNING[79]

"A very pretty wedding occurred Wednesday, Feb. 11, 1914 at high noon at the home of Mr. and Mrs. Peter Rush, when their daughter, Sylvia G. Glendenning, was given in marriage to Mr. John I. Lay. As the wedding march was played by Miss Ollie Rush of Mt. Ayr, the bride and groom took their place under a beautifully draped arch and the ceremony knitting the two lives into one was performed by Rev. A.M. Eastman, their pastor, in the presence of seventy guests."

---

[78] Friend Rush was the oldest child of Sirestus Rush and Margaret Rush (Aunt Jeda). Sirestus Rush was the brother of Peter Rush, Sylvia's stepfather. Friend was born in 1888 and had two younger siblings, a sister, Olive Rush (1890-1987) and Howard M. Rush (1894-1957). Friend Rush married Lillian L. (Malone). Olive Rush married Thomas J. (Ballew) and Howard Rush married Stellia (DeFenbaugh).

[79] Wedding announcement in the Mount Ayr paper in February 1914.

"After the ceremony, the glad hand and best wishes for the future of the happy couple was extended by all. The guests then retired to the sumptuous feast which had been prepared for the occasion. The afternoon soon wiled away in sweet and jovial fellowship so that not only for the nuptial couple but for all it was a most pleasant day and one to be remembered. This praiseworthy young couple have always lived in the near vicinity and is held in the highest esteem."

"The bride is a young lady of rare accomplishments. In the past year she has been demonstrating her ability as an exceptionally successful schoolteacher. Her genial personality has won for her a host of warm friends."

"The groom is a young man of strong personal character; one of real worth. He has always lived on the farm and his industry promises a rich future in that occupation."

"The bride was beautifully gowned in cream silk crepe de chine., trimmed in shadow lace. The groom was handsomely attired in blue serge. The happy couple will be at home to their many friends after March 1, 1914, on the L.C. Lay farm north of Mount Ayr. A wide circle of friends join in extending best wishes for a happy and prosperous journey through life."

The Shot Gun Chivarari

We looked for folks to come to chivarari us, but it was too stormy. A few nights later, after we had gone to bed, they came. The room we were sleeping in had an outside door on two sides. Uncle Sim[80] started to force a door to open, but John grabbed a chair and struck at him. He hit the door and made a dent. They put a gun on the windowsill and shot some shingles off the edge of the roof. We finally got dressed and treated the bunch. Mother knew they were coming, but she didn't want to tell. She hinted that I should not go to bed so early, but I didn't get what she meant.

The Blizzard

On Thursday, the day after the wedding, we had a bad blizzard. Then the next day, Veda and Luella[81] had a dinner for us. They had invited a few more relatives, but not many could get there because the snow was so deep. Because

---

[80] Uncle Sim is Sim C. Rice, the husband of Eva Steadman, Sylvia's aunt.
[81] Veda and Luella were sisters of John Lay. Veda (Oveda) Lay was born June 12, 1877 and died December 12, 1963. She never married. Luella May Lay married Eric Anderson. She was born September 19, 1887 and died July 14, 1954. They had two children: Anna Jane Anderson and Helen Luella Anderson.

grandpa and grandma Steadman could not come, we went over to their house and stayed a day or two.

THE LAY FAMILY

When Sylvia married into the Lay family, she nearly doubled her family size. John Lay was one of nine children of Luther Clark Lay and Sarah Jane (Irving). All nine children were born on the Lay farm in Washington Township. All but one were buried in Ringgold County.

The oldest was Mary Lay (Parker), born January 6, 1876 and died August 15, 1954. She married Lewis Henry Parker (B 2/18/1878 & D 11/2/1951). They had six children:

- Louella Grace Parker   (B 9/13/1904 & D 11/13/1969)
- Mary Pearl Parker   (B 2/25/1906 & D 6/30/1964)
- Glen Parker   (B 6/13/1906 & D 4/7/1909)
- Florence Ruth Parker   (B 10/12/1910 & D 8/17/1974)
- Gladys Lorene Parker   (B 1/13/1913 & D ?)
- Mildred Jane Parker   (B 11/18/1915 & D ?)

Eighteen months later, Oveda was born on June 12, 1877 and she died on December 12, 1963. She remained unmarried.

Then 14 months later Homer Luther Lay was born on August 5, 1879 and died on October 11, 1969. He married Anna PRATT. They had three children:

- Luther Clark Lay   (B 5/17/1908 & D ?)
- Wilbur Lee Lay   (B 4/13/1912 & 9/27/1983)
- Blanch Elizabeth Lay   (B 1918 & D 1918)

The fourth child, Abner Lee Lay, was born 18 months later on April 5, 1881 and he died on January 12, 1962. He remained unmarried.

The fifth child, Corwin Turner Lay, was born on March 5, 1883 and died on March 21, 1962 in Buda, IL. He never married.

The sixth child, Joseph A. Lay, was born on December 5, 1884 and died on April 23, 1959. He never married either.

Nearly three years later the seventh child was born, Luella May Lay, on September 19, 1887 and died on July 14, 1951. She married Eric Anderson (B 3/19/1886 and D June 1940). They had two children:

- Anna Jane Anderson   (B 11/15/1918 & D ?)
- Helen Luella Anderson   (B 8/11/1921 & D ?)

It would be a little over four years later that the eighth child, John L. Lay, was born on November 16, 1891 and died on April 7, 1969. They had two children:

- Robert Glenn Lay   (B 12/27/1916 & D 1990)
- Paul Edward Lay   (B 10/10/1923 & D 1/26/2011)

The last and ninth child, Sari I. Lay, was born on December 12, 1892; however, she would die at the age of two on February 15, 1895.

Sylvia knew all of John's siblings and their spouses; they all lived in Ringgold County at the time she was married to John, and they were all married before John except Luella, who was married seven months later. All of John's siblings lived into their 70's and 80's. John's father, Luther, lived to be 90 and his mother 60.

8

Up on the Farm

1914-1916

Sylvia and John would move on to Luther Lay's family farm (picture below) for the first two years of their married life. They, however, would not enjoy those years alone; they would have a number of people living with them—the most memorable was Corwin, John's brother, who lived with them the first year and left a lasting impression. The second year of marriage would bring the news of another boarder that would change their lives.

The Luther Lay Farm

The Honeymoon Hotel

We drove from my parent's home in the wagon loaded with our furniture. It was eleven miles and a very cold day. We moved our few belongings to the Lay farm, 4 miles north and a half-mile west of Mt. Ayr. Joe[82] helped.

The View of the Lay Farm from the House[83]

We loaded what I had and stopped in town and picked up what we had bought. We had a wagon full. I bought a dishpan big enough for a tub. We got up to the farm almost at night. Homer and Anna[84] had moved out of the house. Anna took the children on to her mother's and Homer finished the moving. He left straw all over the floors where they had put it under the carpet to keep the floors warm. In those days, most people put straw under the carpet. In the spring, they would take up the carpet, wash it, and take the straw out.

In the fall, they would put in new straw after the threshing was done. It was too late to do cleaning that night, so we just set up the bed in the living room

---

[82] Joseph Lay, the brother of John Lay, was born on December 5, 1884 and died on April 23, 1959. He was never married.

[83] The Luther Lay farm was in the Washington Township #13, on 190th street, just west of 220th avenue. (See *Ringgold County 1894 Iowa Historical Atlas*).

[84] Homer Lee Lay, John's brother, was one of nine children by Luther C. Lay and Sarah Jane (Irving). Homer married Anna Elizabeth (Pratt). They had three children: Luther Clark, Wilbur, and Blanch. Homer was born on August 5, 1879 and died on October 11, 1969. Anna was born on March 18, 1879 and died in December of 1969. They along with their three children are buried at the Hickory Grove Cemetery.

so we could clean the bedroom and put carpet down. That night the plaster on the ceiling wall decided to come down right on our bed. We had plaster all over. The next day the straw came out of the house. I had bought a rug for the living room and put my new rag carpet in the bedroom.

The house on the Lay farm was to the right of the tree at the top of the hill.

Missing Elbows

The boys were putting up the cook stove, yet we were short an elbow. There we were at night, 4.5 miles from town, and no working cook stove. So John went to a neighbor's house, the Dants, three fourths of a mile away. They didn't have an extra elbow, but they took one out of the pipe in the washhouse. They were wonderful neighbors all the time we lived by them.

The Extra Roommates

John's mother (Sarah Jane)[85] had passed away before this time (the wedding). John's Dad said we could live on his farm north of Mt. Ayr if Corwin[86] could

[85] Sara Jane (Irving) Lay was born on March 22, 1851 and died on August 11, 1911, two and a half years before Sylvia and John were married. Luther would remain a widow for nearly 22 years until his death in 1933.
[86] Corwin Turner Lay, a brother of John Lay, was born on March 5, 1883 and died on March 21, 1962. He never married.

live with us and he and John farm together. So he lived with us the first year of our married life.

That fall (1914), a teacher, Clara Wiley, came to board with us. She went home on the weekends. The schoolhouse was about ½ mile from our house, the school where John started to school before the family moved to Missouri.

THE SCHOOL HOUSE[87]

When John Lay was in elementary school (1897-1903), he would walk west on this road (towards the foreground) to the school located next to the tree in the foreground (photo right). The Luther Lay farm was located on 190th Street just beyond the top of the hill to the left in Washington Township. The school was located in front of the grove of trees to the right of the road.

Later, when Paul Lay was born on the farm, he would attend the same school and walk down the same road just as his father.

John used the McGuffey's Primer while in school. The Primer is a "...series of schoolbooks teaching reading and moral precepts, originally prepared by William Holmes McGuffey in 1836. McGuffey was a professor at Miami University in Oxford, Ohio, and a Presbyterian minister. A Cincinnati publishing firm asked him to compile a series of graded readers adapted to the values, beliefs, and way of life of 'Western people.' As a young schoolmaster, McGuffey had used the eighteenth-century Puritans' New England Primer, Noah Webster's American Spelling Book, and

---

[87] The schoolhouse was in the Washington Township #24, on the corner of 190th St. and 210th Av. (See *Ringgold County 1984 Iowa Historical Atlas*).

the Bible."[88]

On the inside cover of the book, John traced his hand, wrote his name, and the date, September 14, 1896—three years after Sylvia was born (photo below left). John wrote this warning: "Do not steel this book for the owner caries a pocket knife." (photo below right).

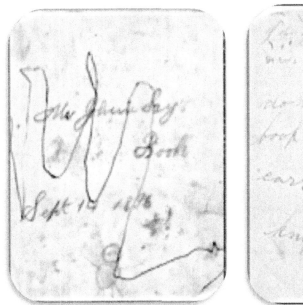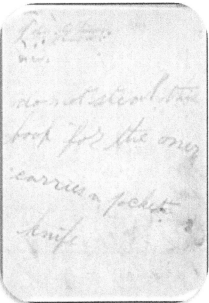

SARAH JANE IRVING LAY

About two and a half years before Sylvia married John Lay, John's mother, Sarah Jane, passed away. At the time of her death, Sylvia most likely did not know that one day she would marry Sarah Jane's son, John Lay. Sarah Jane Irving Lay's obituary is listed below.[89]

"Sarah Jane IRVING was born in Columbus, Ohio, March 22nd, 1851, and died at her home in Ringgold County, Iowa, August 11, 1911, aged sixty years, four months and twenty days. She was the daughter of Charles and Jane IRVING, and the first of eight children they reared to pass away. From Guerensey county, Ohio, she moved with the family to southern Illinois in 1861 and from there to Ringgold county, Iowa, in 1865. She made her home continuously from that time till her death in Ringgold County with the exception of a short time in Missouri."

---

[88] Houghton Mifflin College Division http://mcguffeyreaders.com/history.htm.
[89] Mount Ayr Record-News, Tuesday, August 15, 1911.

"She was one of the charter members of the Presbyterian Church in Mount Ayr. She took her letter from that church signed by her father as elder, and united with her husband, with the Methodist church in 1876. She continued a faithful member of the same to her death. She was happily married to Mr. L. C. [Luther Caleb] LAY at her home in this county September 1, 1875. There are eight living children, Mary PARKER, of Buda, Ill., and Oveda, Homer, Lee, Corwin, Joseph, Louella and John. For the last five years Sister LAY has not had the best of health, but has been up and around and able to do the work even up to the morning of the day she died."

"She leaves a devoted husband, her affectionate children, her brothers and sisters and a large circle of friends to mourn her sudden death. They have the fresh memory of her kind ministries in her family and in the social circle in which she moved and to whom she gave all of her heart's love and her hands service. One can scarcely realize that she has gone. It would seem she must return from some other room, or from the garden to be again the center of the happy circle. It will be long before those devoted hearts become adjusted to her departure."

Luther and Sarah (Irving) Lay

Life with Corwin

When Corwin moved in with us, he used a small bedroom. Our house was the only house on a one-mile road. We were eleven miles from the folks. Because Corwin had a driving horse, I would drive down home and to town. John and Corwin farmed some ground away from home, so they took their lunch with them. Consequently, I was alone all day. I was to have help with the washing, but I never saw any. I wasn't used to being waited on like the Lay women were (photo right: Corwin, left, John, right).

Corwin had promised to pay half of the grocery bill, which he never did. My eggs paid most of it. Mother had given me 50 hens and Veda gave us 14, so when we wanted to board the teacher. I figured what the groceries would cost per week. I kept count of what we bought. I figured what half would be, and I told Corwin he could pay that, which was very little. The teacher was only paying $3.00 per week, and I charged nothing for his laundry, but he stayed all winter and wouldn't pay one penny!

Corwin's Ultimatum

The spring (1915), we told him either he or we had to move, so he moved into a little house Uncle Joe Irving[90] owned, and he farmed some of Uncle Joe's land. Corwin left a harrow leaf—that is all we got for a winter's keep! We were now alone so we bought the folks' organ so I spent many hours entertaining myself by playing the organ.

---

[90] Uncle Joe Irving was Joseph L. Irving, the brother of Sarah Jane Irving, the wife of Luther Lay. Joe was born on November 26, 1859 and died on August 17, 1949.

That summer (1915), Corwin and John cut and threshed Uncle Joe's land for a share of it (photo below). Aunt Nellie[91] said to come to her house to cook for the threshers, so I fooled Corwin that time. I charged half of the groceries to him, but I still did the work. Veda and Lowell never helped me do a tap of work all the years that I helped them every time they called.

The Irving Farm[92]

Nell in the Well

Nell (Sylvia's half-sister) wasn't old enough to go to school, and she thought so much of John. She would come and stay with us until mother would make her come home. One morning while she was still in bed, the boys went to the field, and I milked and turned out the cows. We had a well not far from the cow lot, an open well out of which we drew water with a bucket. I had just

[91] Nellie (Price) Irving was married to Joseph Irving. He was born on January 28, 1876 and died on April 3, 1951.
[92] The Irving Farm in the Liberty Township #7 was on the corner of 190th Street and 220th Avenue, less than a half-mile due east of the Luther Lay farm. (See *Ringgold County 1894 Iowa Historical Atlas* Joseph Irving).

opened the gate when I heard the bucket go into the well. I remembered the water bucket in the house was about empty, so the first thing I thought was that Nell had come to the well for water and had fallen in. I was so frightened. I started screaming her name. I yelled so loudly, I awakened her. She came out of the house, rubbing her eyes and asking what I wanted. I was so relieved; I had just experienced a terrible shock. I went over and looked; the bucket had fallen in. Someone had failed to the tie the rope, I suppose. Anyway, Nell was safe, and she had never looked so good to me. She seemed to belong to us. We could have kept her and raise her as our own. Mother said she was getting weaned away from home, so she couldn't stay at our house so much.

JOHN LAY'S MATERNAL GRANDPARENTS:
CHARLES AND MARY (PUGH) IRVING

John Lay's mother, Sarah Jane (Irving) Lay was the daughter of Charles and Mary (Pugh) Irving, John's grandparents. Robert Lay, Sylvia's oldest son, received a letter[93] in 1964 from a granddaughter of Charles and Mary Irving:

"Charles Hood Irving was born in Newton Stewart on the river Foyle in Tyrone co, Ulster, Ireland. I have a card somewhere which came from Uncle Sam Irving, which is the picture of the seat of the Irving clan. It is an old Castle in Scotland, so his people came from there, but I have no dates. Charles came to America and walked from Philadelphia to Columbus, Ohio, where I think he was a carpenter. He and Mary (Pugh) were married there. It must have been about 1849 because your grandmother Jane Lay was about 2 years older than my Mother and the oldest child."

"Mary Pugh Irving was born in Oswestey, Montgomery, Shire Wales. She spoke the Welch language as a child. She had a brother named William who was a fine scholar. She came alone to America as a maid and met my Grandfather (Charles) in Columbus, Ohio and came to Olney, IL, where Uncle George and Aunt Emma Irving Fraser were born. They later came to Iowa and settled in Ringgold County. My uncle said because water was available and the land was inexpensive. They were poor but Christians (Presbyterians). My grandmother would work hard all week and walk to Mt. Ayr to church on Sunday. My mother said she would walk barefooted to town and put on her shoes and stockings before going into church. Their farm was the old Irving farm where Triggs now live."

"My grandfather and grandmother were nice looking. Later she had a black heavy

---

[93]A letter from Maude Henderson, the granddaughter of Charles and Mary Irving on May 24, 1964.

silk bonnet and dress and wore a lovely black shawl. She had a large type Bible, which she kept up on a shelf in the living room. She read it daily in the afternoon. They died in 1895, a week apart in the same house which is now the Triggs farm. Grandmother was not told of grandfather's death, but as soon as it occurred, she, who was very sick with pneumonia, told them that she saw the angel come to get him. They were always 'Father' and 'Mother'".

"My grandfather Irving had thick wavy hair and grandmother's was light color and you could see it all through the Irvings. Ned, George, Hugh and Lowell have light hair. Also Mary Oveda and Joe Lay. Charlie Henderson and I have the thick dark hair. The Irvings were hardworking, honest, and fine citizens."

Charles and Mary Irving: Rose Hill Cemetery, Mt. Ayr, Iowa (2014)

In 1971, Robert Lay received a letter from the wife of a grandson of Charles and Mary Irving[94]:

"Your Great Grandmother Mary (Pugh) Irving was born in Wales, and your Great Grandfather Charles Hood Irving was born in Northern Ireland of Scottish descent. The lived at one time in New York but emigrated west. He (Charles) was a carpenter by trade. They stopped at one time in Ohio, where he worked building the State Capital. He was more of a carpenter than a farmer, leaving much of the farm work to the sons as soon as they were able. Charles Irving was always cheery, out-going and

---

[94] A letter from the wife of Charles Irving Henderson, the grandson of Charles and Mary Irving, on May 27, 1971.

gay. His wife, Mary, was hard working, dour, and withdrawn. She must have been overwhelmed with the responsibility she was forced to accept. She delivered home-made butter and fresh eggs to her town customers, walking to Mt. Ayr."

Bus Driver

In 1916, when I was pregnant with Robert, Aunt Eva and Uncle Sim used to come in their new car and take us for a ride. One Sunday, we went to Creston. We thought it was quite a car ride. Then they began wanting John to go to Delphos and apply for a job as a school bus driver. So finally we decided to go. John got the job for $34 a month. They were starting to build the consolidated school house.

THE DELPHOS SCHOOL, 1916[95]

The city of Delphos voted to consolidate several schools into one new school to be built in Delphos. The three-story building was completed in 1916, and it was located across the street from the Baptist Church.[96] Sylvia's uncle Leonard Steadman and Uncle Sim C. Rice were two of the original board members in 1916. A memorial remains in the city of Delphos today, listing Sylvia's two uncles' names (photos next page).

---

[95] Courtesy of IAGenWeb.org/Ringgold County.
[96] IAGenWeb.org/Ringgold County.

THE DELPHOS CONSOLIDATED SCHOOL (2014)

9

Change is Coming

1916-1919

Life on the Lay farm was short lived. After two and a half years, Sylvia and John would move to the city of Delphos—a town of about 100 people. John would begin a new job, Sylvia would give birth to her first son, and the uncle from Montana would reenter the picture. Sylvia's seventh half-sibling would be born, the family would move back on the farm, a World War would start, a house would burn down, and tragedy would strike again—twice—all within three years.

Hickory Grove Cemetery, Ringgold County, Iowa (2014)

Loneliness of a Bus Driver

We moved in August and John started to drive the bus when school started. We had to get up at 5 am. John left the bus at the end of the route at John Reynold's house. In the morning, he would drive the buggy to Reynold's house, hitch it to the bus, and pick up the kids. During the day, he hauled goods from the depot for Grandpa, and in the evening he took the kids home, left the bus, and came home in the buggy. He would leave in the dark and come home in the dark.[97]

[97] The Reynold's farm was in the Middle Fork Township #4 and was on 290th street, 1 mile east of Co. Highway P32. The Reynold's home was located on the left in the foreground. John Lay would travel up and down this road, 3.5 miles from Delphos driving the school bus. (See *Ringgold County 1915 Ogle Iowa Historical Atlas*).

Living in Town

Uncle Sim and Uncle Leonard helped out, we guessed. Uncle Sim rented us their house in Delphos. They reserved two rooms for themselves, but we still had two bedrooms. They both worked at the store[98] and ate at a Fannie Cooper's boarding house. We didn't sell anything because we didn't have too much to sell. We let a family move in the Lay farmhouse and look after what cows we had. We did take one cow, our hogs for meat, and our chickens.

Left to Right:[99]

Ben Seaton (Sylva's Uncle, married Fannie Steadman),

Sam Seaton,

Sim Rice (Sylvia's Uncle, married Eva Steadman)

In October, on my birthday (21 years old), they had a surprise on me. All the folks, aunts, and uncles, and grandma and grandpa came at once.

Awaiting a New Arrival

I was busy making baby clothes. I put tatting and crocheting on most of the clothes. We lived next door to the Christian church (photo right). One day I was rendering Lard as we

---

[98] The Baker Store was purchased by Sylvia's Grandfather.
[99] Courtesy of Delphos Centennial 1880-1980.

had butchered, and unannounced, the Ladies Aid came and said they wanted to use mine and Aunt Eva's[100] sewing machine. So they worked there all afternoon. On December 24, 1916, I didn't feel good so Uncle Sim went for Aunt Mae. The doctor was called, but it was a false alarm, so he went to bed awhile. There were so many babies that winter that he was tired out. After a while, he got up and said he wasn't needed yet, so he went home. The folks came to our house the next day, Christmas.

On December 27, 1916, Robert was born (photo below). He weighed 8 ½ pounds. Aunt Mae and Aunt Hattie were with me. Every morning at 5 when we got up, the baby wanted up, so I dressed him soon as I got up every morning. Robert kept choking when he ate, so we discovered he was tongue-tied. When he was six weeks old, the doctor clipped his tongue.

---

[100] Aunt Mae was Mae E. (Rice) Steadman, married to Leonard B. Steadman, Sylvia's uncle.

Montana's Visit

Uncle Claude came back for a visit that winter. He came over and stayed with us a few days. Grandma had us all over for supper one evening. Our house where we lived was across the street from grandma and grandpa. It was a much better winter for me there than on the farm in that old cold house with a baby.

HOUSE ACROSS THE STREET

This could be the home Sylvia refers to when she lived in Delphos. This is the house Sylvia's aunt Fannie lived in later in her life. This house sits across from where Sylvia's grandfather's store would have been.

Back to the Farm

But we became anxious to get back on a farm, so John rented a farm 2.5 miles north of Mt. Ayr, from Frank Gleason.[101] When Robert was two months old, March 1917, we moved. We had kept our chickens and stock. The baby and I stayed with the folks while John moved the furniture. Aunt Hattie had come and helped me pack. John got everything in the house and straightened up

---

[101] The farm was located north of Highway 2 in the Washington Township #5, west of State Highway 66. Sylvia said the farm was 2.5 miles north of Mt. Ayr; this farm is 4.5 miles west according to the 1915 farm maps. This is the only Gleason farm found within a 5-mile radius of Mt. Ayr. (See *Ringgold County 1915 Ogle Iowa Historical Atlas* F.E. Gleason).

before I got there. Olive and Tommy[102] were at mother's in a car, so they took me up to the farm as they went home so I wouldn't have to keep the baby out so long. We worked very hard on the farm we had rented from Gleason. We were paying cash rent. We lived there two years (photo below).

Adventures with Robert

Aunt Jeda[103] and Hattie were scuffling over some fudge Hattie was saving for her beaux. They accidentally hit the baby basket and upset it. Mother ran and picked up Robert and said,

"Now you have killed the baby."

She examined him and didn't tell us until later that he had quite a bump on

[102] Olive G. (Rush) was the daughter of Sirestus M. Rush, Peter Rush's brother. She married Thomas Jefferson Ballew. Olive was born on May 20, 1890 and died on May 25, 1987. Thomas was born in 1892 and died in 1973.
[103] Aunt Jeda is Margaret (Anderson) Rush, married to Sirestus Rush, the brother of Peter Rush. Aunt Hattie was Hattie Irene (Steadman) Geiger, married to Ed Geiger.

the back of his head. The basket had tipped with his head first. He didn't fall out of the basket but hit his head on the basket. We soon discovered the house we had moved into was so cold as the old farmhouse north and west of Mr. Ayr. The house was small. The bedroom was off the living room and the living room was very small. The room off the kitchen was too cold to use in the winter. The upstairs only had an unfinished attic. There was no bathroom or any convenience of any kind. I had to carry water from a well down in the field and crawl through a barbed wire fence.

FOUR GENERATIONS

Standing:

Sylvia (Glendenning) Lay

Sitting (L to R):

Delia (Willey) Steadman,

Robert Glen Lay,

Mary O. (Steadman) Glendenning Rush

One day I went for a bucket of water and left Robert alone. He was crawling now or really sliding on his bottom, which is the way he crawled. I got to the fence with my bucket of water. As I was getting through the fence, I upset the bucket, so I had to go back and get another bucket. When I got to the house, Robert had opened the cupboard door and was trying to drink the cake coloring.

Robert Lay (1918)

We got a big wooden box and I lined it. John would tip it up by the stove and warm it well. When Robert was about one year old, he would play in the box while I did chores. I would carry Robert and go after the cows then either put him in a box by the cow lot or hold him on my lap while I milked.

Robert Lay (1918)

Shopping Spree

When the year was over, we didn't have enough to pay the cash rent. We had to borrow until we could sell the hogs in the spring. Grandpa Glendenning's estate had been settled, so I got my money during the spring. I bought a Jersey cow from Uncle Curt Abarr and John needed another horse so he bought a horse. Then we bought a Model T car from Uncle Sim, and John taught me to drive (photo right: a sample Model T[104]).

Fire on the Farm

Corwin had moved on the home place again (The Lay farm) where we had left. That spring the house burned down. The only thing he saved was our telephone, which we had left on the wall. They built a small house with insurance.

World War I Baby

In April this year, 1917, Arthur was born (photo right) mother's eighth child. He was a very cross baby all summer. The war was in full swing. John was called for his exam, but he didn't pass because he was flat-footed. They also were not taking fathers. Because flour was rationed, a man would come and check to see how much flour you had on hand. We didn't have coupons; they just took your word or looked for themselves. So we baked bread with oatmeal, corn meal, and rice meal. Aunt Vicki Irving[105] told me to make mush out of corn meal and put it in the bread dough. It was the best bread I made; it

---

[104] Public Domain.
[105] Aunt Vicki Irving was married to John A. Irving, the brother of Sarah Irving, the mother of John Lay. Vicki was born on August 16, 1864 and died on March 5, 1958. John Irving was born on February 13, 1857 and died on November of 1943.

was light and good. We used Karo syrup in place of sugar in making ice cream.

Death Visits the Family

It was in that summer after we moved from Delphos that Grandpa Steadman went to the hospital. He discovered he had cancer of the liver. He passed away in August, 1917. Then Uncle Leonard moved in with Grandma for a year; they then moved back to the farm and Aunt Fannie and Uncle Ben Seaton moved in and lived with her until her death.

GRANDPA STEADMAN'S OBITUARY[106]

"John S. Steadman passed away Friday, August 24th, 1917 at his home in Delphos, Iowa, aged 70 years, 6 months, and 25 days. Mr. Steadman was born in Noble County, Ohio, January 29, 1847 and came to Guthrie County, Iowa in 1870. On February 6, 1873, he was united in marriage to Miss Delia Willey and for two years the young couple made their home in Guthrie County. He came to Ringgold County and settled at his old home in the Hickory Grove Community, where he resided until about 15 years ago when he became a citizen of Delphos, engaging in the mercantile business in which he continued until the time of his death"

"Mr. Steadman was a man of unimpeachable character and sterling qualities, ever stimulating and upholding righteousness in the communities in which he lived."

"In his early life he was a member of the Methodist Episcopal Church and later in life united with the Adventist Christian Church at Hickory Grove in which he ever lived a consistent Christian life, an honor to the church and an inspiration of righteousness to all who knew

---
[106] Mt. Ayr Paper, August 1917.

him. The church he loved and the community in which he lived sustain an irreparable loss in his death, bringing upon them a sadness and gloom dispelled only by the thought that our world has been made better and our lives richer because he has lived and the hope that we shall meet him again in that other and better land where death shall be a stranger and sorrow, pains, and tears forever gone."

"Mr. Steadman leaves to mourn his loss a wife and six children—Mrs. Peter Rush (Sylvia's mother), Mrs. J.M. Addison, Mrs. B.F. Seaton, Mrs. Ed Geiger, Mrs. S.C. Rice, and Mr. L.B. Steadman, all of Delphos. Mr. Steadman was of a family of fourteen children, of which six sisters and four brothers survive him. Funeral services were conducted in the Hickory Grove Chapel by Rev. T. E. Glendenning. Interment was made in Hickory Grove cemetery."

Death Visits Again

When we got the word Aunt Eva would have the second operation, Mother and Aunt Connie (Alice)[107] went to St. Joe MO. on the train. Mother had Arthur with her. Grandma was already down there, and I think the other girls too. Uncle Leonard was in Des Moines at the State Fair. We went to his home and as soon as he came, Leonard, John, I, along with Robert, started to drive to St. Joe. We didn't know the way. It was at night and the route was marked by painted stripes on telephone poles. We would stop, get out with a flashlight and look at the poles.

We finally got there, but when we got to the hospital, Aunt Eva had passed away at the age of 34. The family had left the hospital. We didn't find them until later in the day. Mother's cousin lived in St. Joe. She and her family wanted to go to Delphos to the funeral but didn't think they could afford to all go on the train. So Uncle Leonard asked John to drive home and the family to ride with him, so Uncle Leonard and I went on the train with the rest of the family.

Grandma had torn down her house and was building a new one and Aunt Eva and Uncle Sim were going to live with her, so they took Aunt Eva's body to Uncle Leonard's. Back then, no one ever heard of leaving a body in the funeral home.

---

[107] Aunt Connie was also known as Sarah Alice Steadman, the sister of Sylvia's mother, Mary Ollie.

AUNT EVA'S OBITUARY

"Eva Gertrude Stedman was born in Ringgold County, Iowa, January 7, 1884, and died at the Ensworth Hospital in St. Joseph, MO August 27, 1918, aged thirty-four years, seven months and twenty days. She was married to S.C. Rice of Delphos, Iowa, January 5, 1908. She was the youngest daughter of Mr. and Mrs. J. S. Stedman. She became a Christian in early life, uniting with the Adventist Christian Church of which she remained a faithful member until the time of her death."

"Although being too far removed to do active work in her own church, she took pleasure in working with her husband in the Christian church. She leaves to mourn her death her husband, mother, four sisters, and one brother, besides a host of friends. The funeral service was held from the Christian church in Delphos, conducted by Rev. W. C. Williams of Diagonal, and the body was laid in Rose Hill cemetery at Mount Ayr. "

"Card of Thanks: We take this means of expressing to our many neighbors and friends our heart-felt thanks for their acts of kindness and the sympathy expressed in words of comfort and generous help during the illness and on the occasion of the death and funeral of our wife and daughter."

Eva Gertrude Steadman,
Rosehill Cemetery, Mt. Ayr, Iowa (2014)

10

Mystery of Life

1919-1927

Sylvia and John were on the move again, moving five times within the next eight years. Their American dream would be threatened by the frailty of life. The family would share the joy of new life and the mystery of an old life.

Rice Township (2013)

Peter Rush's Farm Again

After we had been on the Gleason farm for two years, Dad decided he wanted to move to town. He said he would rent us his farm. We moved there in March, 1919, and the folks moved to Mt. Ayr. Mother sold her 40 acres she inherited from Grandpa and bought the home.

An original building on a farm next to Peter Rush's farm

The house was not modern with no paint on the outside of the house, but it was better than the one we had been in before. We had a sink in the kitchen, a well by the door, and a nice big cellar under the house. We were beginning to get some stock and all our calves were heifers, so we thought we soon would have a lot of milk cows. We had a good crop along with several little lambs. I raised quite a few chickens, and I raised a big garden. I canned lots of food~ canned 100 quarts of tomatoes, besides beans, corn and fruit. We were doing very well.

Illinois or Bust

We had not had a vacation in the over two years we had been married. We had bought a new car that fall, so we decided to drive to John's sister, Mary[108], and her family, in Illinois (The city of Buda, in Bureau County). Homer and Anna decided to go too, so we both started out in our Model T Ford.

THE MODEL T[109]

The Ford Model T, built between 1908 and 1927, became known as the car for the "common man". Known as the "Tin Lizzie", the Model T sold for $300 by 1925, comprising about 40% of all of the cars sold in the United States. The 20 horsepower engine allowed the car to reach top speeds of 40-45 miles per hour. The car had a 10-gallon fuel tank and was started by a hand crank until after the 1920 models. Until 1925, only one color was offered—black.

Mary and Lewis Parker lived in the village of Buda, Illinois, in the Concord Township in Bureau, County, about 300 miles from Mt. Ayr and 117 miles southwest of Chicago. By 1910, Buda had a population 887.

If we averaged 25 miles per hour, we thought we had done very well. The trip

[108] Mary Elizabeth Lay was the oldest child of Luther and Sarah Lay. She was born on January 6, 1876 and died on August 16, 1954. Mary married Lewis Parker and they had five children: Louella Grace, Mary Pearl, Florence Ruth, Gladys Lorine, and Mildred Jane.
[109] Picture public domain.

took us two whole days to drive. We started early, and at night we stopped at a farm and camped in a barn lot. We had a stack cover which we tried to make into a tent. We got hay from the farmer and spread blankets on it for a bed. Homer, Anna, Wilbur, Clark, John, Robert, and I were all in one little tent. We had quite a storm during the night. Robert was so afraid because it was his first night sleeping out. He wasn't quite 3 yet. We had a nice visit while there. John went on the train to Chicago to visit a second cousin. Robert and I stayed at Mary's home. The weather was so hot, I was afraid Robert would get sick, so I gave up going. Coming home it took us two and half days. We had an old couple stay and do the chores while we were gone.

SYLVIA'S NIECES: THE PARKER GIRLS FROM 1917

Back Row: (L to R) Louella, Mary, Florence

Middle: Gladys

Front: Mildred

The American Dream

Dad decided that winter (1919) to sell the farm, which meant another move, so we decided to have a sale, sell part of our stock and sell the car and buy a farm. Uncle John Irving would loan us the money and take a mortgage. We were buying the old Funkhauser place. John was to meet Renzie Funkhauser in town and give him a $1,000 note. Joe needed to go to the hospital for a minor operation and Wilbur had to have something done.

THE FUNKHAUSER FARM[110]

It is unclear where this farm was located. According to the 1915 Ringgold County farm map, a farm owned by G. H. Funkhauser was close to Peter Rush's farm. The Funkhauser farm was in the Poe Township east of 24th avenue between 270th street to the north and 280th street to the south. The Funkhauser farm was only 4 miles from Peter Rush's farm. Because the Funkhauser farm was in the general area of where Sylvia and John were living, and the farm was adjoining to the Sutherland farm, this may be the farm they were going to purchase.

So John was elected to go, but he told them he had to meet this man for a business deal and couldn't go. I pleaded with him not to go, but they told him

[110] See *Ringgold County 1915 Ogle Iowa Historical Atlas.*

he had to or they wouldn't take Joe and it would be his fault. So John went but it was when the flu was so bad. He came home one evening, went to town the next day and gave the $1,000 note to Funkhauser.

Three Generations of Lay Family (1919)
L to R: Luther Lay, Robert Lay, John Lay

Death of a Dream

Then the next day John came down with the flu. Although Robert and I took the flu from him, John's flu ran into pneumonia then abscessed on his lung. After he was sick for several weeks, we took him to St. Joe hospital where he had surgery on February, 1920. No one, not even our doctor, expected him to come home alive. I stayed with John in the hospital. Lee[111], however, was going to have a sale for us; he wanted to sell everything. Lee said,

"John isn't coming back."

John begged Lee not to sell his black team. One of them he had bought when I got my money. I said no; he could not sell the Jersey cow and my chickens. I had worked too hard, and they were laying well. So Veda took the hens, cut off their tails, and turned them in with hers, and she sent me egg money. John was very bad; he had a special nurse night and day. We were there 3 weeks, and there went our $1,000. After Funkhauser heard of John's illness and knew he couldn't work for a year, he tore up the note.

Lee Lay with the Parker Girls

Oklahoma Bound

When we came from the hospital, we stayed at my folks until May of 1920. We had been told by the nurse that John should go south (Oklahoma) for the winter. We went down but were not happy there. We stayed two weeks and decided to go back to the farm. Our furniture was all stored in one room of the house on the farm.

---

[111] Lee Lay is the brother of John Lay.

Bed Bugs

We then rented the house that was known as the Hiss Willey[112] house about 2 miles east from Dad's farm (photo below). We discovered it was full of bed bugs. It was my first experience with bugs. I fought them all summer. We had a little pasture and a very small piece for corn. We paid $6.00 per month. Our eggs and cream kept us and also bought us another cow. We spent a happy summer there.

The Sutherland Farm

In the fall that year (1920), John was improving so fast that Clyde Sutherland[113] wanted us to stay and do their chores and can the peaches while

---

[112] The Willey place was on the corner of 270th street and 220th avenue in the Rice Township #25. (See *Ringgold County 1894 Iowa Historical Atlas*).

[113] Clyde Sutherland's farm was in the Poe Township #33 on 270th street, between 240th avenue to the west and 250th street to the east. (See *Ringgold County 1915 Ogle Iowa Historical Atlas*). Clyde was born on November 14, 1877 and died on February 25, 1934. He was married to Leota (Olney) and he was the son of Jonathon and Permelia Sutherland.

they took a trip. So we got the same couple that had stayed the year before to do our chores, and we went to the Sutherlands. I canned 100 quarts of peaches for her. We had a whole bunch of cows to milk also.

The Sutherland Farm

Return to the Lay Farm

Corwin was going to go to Minnesota, so we decided to move back on the home place north of Mt. Ayr. On October 1920, we went back. Since we first lived there, the old house had burned down. They built a new house—two small rooms down and two up. We didn't have the rats to fight as we had when we first lived there. We were lucky we took no bed bugs with us. Before we moved, I poured gasoline all over the mattresses. We also dug a well close to the house. John built a small screened porch by the kitchen, which helped as we put the cream separator in it. He used boards from boxes to board it up part way. We had to buy stock and start over again. The next year a teacher boarded with us.

The Lay Brothers

In the spring (1922), Robert, age 5, started to school for a few weeks. He had been vaccinated for smallpox, so he only went three weeks. We bought used lumber in town and built a hen house. When Robert was about six years old (1922), we thought he should have a brother or sister. If something would happen to him, we would have no child. So the next year on October 10, 1923, Paul was born. He weighed 11 pounds. We were proud of our boys and very happy.

Paul and Robert Lay (1923)

UNEXPECTED DEATH

Two months before Paul Lay was born, Sylvia's first cousin, Homer Lay, committed suicide. Homer's father was Lewis Lay, the brother of Luther Lay, the father of Sylvia's husband, John Lay. The newspaper article describes the death below.

"SICK OF LIFE; NOBODY CARED / Augusta Suicide left Good-by note—had planned suicide for some time. Augusta, Aug 22 (1923)"

" 'I'm sick of life. Good-by to all my friends. Nobody cares for me but Jesus.' were the contents of a note left by Homer Lay of Augusta, who committed suicide Monday by taking a large dose of strychnine. He obtained the poison at the Augusta drug store, telling the clerk that he wished to kill off the sparrows around his house."

"Lyall James, employer of Lay since the latter came to the village last March, when Lay did not come to work as usual, went to his home to investigate and found him lying on his bed. The note expelling the reason for his act, and orders to call up the Spaulding undertaking home in Battle Creek, was found on the table. It is understood that he had had the details of his act arranged for some time, even to the purchasing of the casket."

"Lay, who is 65 years of age, former of Battle Creek, was last seen about 11 o'clock Monday morning when he was working around the outbuildings. In the afternoon, Roy Taylor, manager of the Augusta lumber yards, went to locate him to collect an account. He knocked on the door but received no answer. His suspicions aroused, Taylor looked in the window and saw Lay on the bed, but thought him to be asleep."

"That was about 2 o'clock in the afternoon. Lyall James found him in the position at 5 o'clock. He had evidently been dead for four or five hours. The sheriff and coroner of Kalamazoo took charge of the body."

"Lay evidently intended for some time to take his life, as three weeks ago he told a neighbor, Albert Broberg, to keep a close watch on the house. He also told Broberg that he would very much like to have an old friend of his in East LeRoy conduct his funeral services when he died. And, if it were impossible to secure this friend, Lay request that the Rev. W. C. Flowerday of Augusta conduct the services. Lay has distant relatives in Battle Creek. Funeral arrangements have not yet been completed." (June 1858-August 20,1923 / West Leroy Cemetery, West Leroy, Michigan). [114]

Move to Mt. Ayr

Then when Paul was about two years old (1925), my nerves were about to break, so we decided the next fall to move to town. John would sell NcNess goods, so when Paul was about 3 (Fall 1926), we moved to Mt. Ayr. Robert was in the 6th grade at school. We lived in Mt. Ayr during the winter of 1926-27, next door to Hattie, Charlie, and Donald.[115] Hattie worked at the store, and Donald stayed with us after school until his mother got home. One day I looked out and Paul (photo right) had his wagon piled full of something. I called and said,

"What are you doing?"

"I am moving back to the 'sarm'.

He sometimes didn't talk plain.

---

[114] Augusta, Michigan Newspaper, August 22, 1928.

[115] Hattie (Rush) Jackson is the half-sister of Sylvia. They had a son named Donald.

THE CITY OF MT. AYR

In the fall of 1926, Sylvia and John and their two sons moved off of the Lay farm in the Washington Township and moved to the city of Mt. Ayr, four miles south of the Lay farm. Although Sylvia had lived in town while she attended high school in 1909-1911, this is the first time she lived in town and not on a farm. Sylvia and John lived in Mt. Ayr for six months during the winter of 1926/1927 and then returned to the farm in the spring of 1927. They lived two more times in Mt. Ayr, both times during the winter months and both times for about six months each (winter of 1929-1930 and winter of 1931-1932).

Mt. Ayr had existed as an incorporated town for just over fifty years before Sylvia and John moved there. The town was named "*Mount* because it was the highest elevation between the Mississippi and Missouri Rivers, and *Ayr* after the birthplace of the poet Robert BURNS, Ayr, Scotland."[116]

The same year Sylvia and John moved to town in 1926, the fourth courthouse (photo above) was approved by the voters and was built at a cost of $132,533.[117] The courthouse is still in use as of 2016.

Because the new courthouse included a jail, the original jail, built in 1895, was sold to be used as a memorial for World War I soldiers. It is listed on the National Register of Historical Places[118] (photo next page).

---

[116] "History of Mount Ayr, Ringgold County Iowa" http://iagenweb.org/ringgold/history/mtayr/hist-mountayr.html.

[117] Ringgold County Courthouse, Mount Ayr. http://iagenweb.org/ringgold/.

[118] Ringgold County History Notes. http://iagenweb.org/ringgold/history/misc/hist-historynotes.html.

Fourteen years before Sylvia was born, the railroad came to Mt. Ayr in 1879. The train depot (photo below) was remolded in 1917. In 1968, the depot closed and was converted to a museum in 2000.[119]

The city hall was built in 1918 (photo below), eight years before Sylvia and John moved, and it was remolded with the rounded corner in 1940, five years after they moved out of Ringgold County. [120]

[119] Mt. Ayr Museum Depot. http://iagenweb.org/ringgold/history/misc/his-museum_histsoc.html.
[120] http://iagenweb.org/ringgold/history/mtayr/hist_princessMAcityhall.htm.

Across the street from the city hall was the Princess Theater, having been moved to its location in 1914. A 1920 photo, taken in front of the Princess Theater, includes pictures of some people John and Sylvia most likely knew (photo below). [121]

Princess Theater, Mt. Ayr, Iowa (2011)

[121] Mt. Ayr Record News. http://iagenweb.org/ringgold/history/mtayr/hist_princessMAcityhall.htm.

When Sylvia and John moved to Mt. Ayr in 1926, the population was 1728, about the same number as today.[122]

A view from the southeast side of the square, looking west.
This building was built in 1880 (2011)

Skip Day

One day Robert didn't want to go to school. He said he would have to sing and the kids would laugh at him. So I went with him and talked to his music teacher, Pearl Maple. She said Robert Hudson had made fun the day before. I guess they were laughing with him, and Robert thought they were laughing at him. That is the last time he asked to miss school.

---

[122] Mt. Ayr, Iowa https://en.wikipedia.org/wiki/Mount_Ayr, Iowa.

11

On the Move

1927-1935

The next eight years Sylvia and John would move eight times, moving back and forth between the farm and the city, trying to make a living in both places. There would be another move that at the time was expected but later it would have an unexpected result on the family.

Farm North of Tingley, Iowa (2014)

Two Farms

In the spring of 1927, we bought cows, hogs, and hens from George Kimball and moved back on the Lay farm because the selling of NcNess products wasn't profitable. We lived there until Paul was 4, then we moved on a farm up by Tingley (March 1928). We lived there one year. Robert went to the Tingley school in the 7th grade.

The Tingley Farm:

Owned by the Irving Family[123] (2014)

Public School in Tingley, Iowa (2014)

---

[123] The farm was owned by George W. Irving in the Tingley Township on the southwest corner of #21, on the corner of 140th street and 240th avenue. (See *Ringgold County 1915 Ogle Iowa Historical Atlas* George W. Irving).

Lay Farm Sold

We lived there one year as the farm was sold. We again had built up a nice bunch of stock, but I wasn't well, so the doctor said to travel. So we again had a sale in January of 1929 and then we drove to Idaho in the spring of 1929.

John and Sylvia in Idaho
It was most likely taken on a visit to Idaho after 1929.

Kate's Place

We came back from Idaho in August of 1929 and rented a house in Mt. Ayr from Kate Primmer, across from Roy Miller's place. It was full of rats in the basement. John worked for XT Prentis at the hatchery.

PRENTIS HATCHERY[124]

XT Prentis operated the hatchery in Mount Ayr and a feed business for 54 years. He would later serve in the Iowa House of Representatives from 1939 to 1947. He was

---

[124] Fanflower's Weblog http://fanflower.com/tag/percy-prentis/.

born September 2, 1896 and died October 9, 1978. The Prentis Hatchery was started by XT Prentis in 1924. It had a capacity of 2,400 eggs and by 1936, it had increased to 100,000. The hatchery was later operated by his son, Richard, and finally by Richard's son-in-law.

Gleason's Farm Again

Frank Gleason (the same one) talked us into moving on his farm, just west of Fred Barker's farm on the old highway. He was building all new buildings. He said John could still work for XT but we soon found out he couldn't do two jobs, especially when I wasn't any help.

The Gleason Farm (2011)

I was so poorly that we kept help to do the housework. I couldn't seem to do anything. I went to Iowa City to the doctor. John worked in the field and took care of both boys. Mother did the washing and ironing, helping all she could.

The Long Place

After I came home from Iowa City, we decided to keep John's dad, Luther. He was in town paying people (The DeHarts) to keep him. So we rented a house in town, Mt. Ayr, in the fall of 1931. It was the old Long place, just up south from the folks.

North of Miller's Place

Eric Anderson (photo right)[125], however, went and was appointed guardian of John's Dad and wouldn't let Luther come to stay with us. So in the spring of 1932, we rented a place on the corner just north of Joe Miller's, where the highway turned south, just west of Mr. Ayr (photo below).[126]

John cashed his insurance policy to buy stock again, but we never did get a bunch of stock like we had before the last sale. This house was cold. One of the rooms we couldn't use in the winter, and again we had to carry water. Paul went to a country school close by, and Robert was in high school. He either walked or caught a ride for the 3 miles to Mt. Ayr.

---

[125] Eric Anderson was the husband of Luella May Lay, John's sister. Eric was born March 19, 1886 and died in June of 1940. The photo is of Eric Anderson and his wife, Luella (Lay).

[126] The farm was on the corner of 228th street, just north of present day highway 2 in Rice Township #3. The house is the original one Sylvia and John lived in back in 1932. Picture 2014. (See *Platt Book of Ringgold County Iowa 1930* D.H. Caldwell).

After one year, the insurance man who we rented from wanted to move on another place about ½ mile east on the south side of the road. This was because there was more land near that he could rent then the one we were on, but John couldn't handle that much land.

The Nichols Place

So, in the spring of 1933, we moved on a farm—the Old Nichols Place[127] west of where we lived on the Gleason farm. I was just at the top of the hill west of Uncle Curt Abarr's place. I walked and carried an old hen setting on her eggs. Although the lady moving out left it clean, even washing the windows, the house itself was bad. The one room off of the kitchen is how the rats got in; they were thick outside.

The Old Nichols Place

---

[127] The Nichols farm was in the Rice Township # 7 just east of Benton on the south side of Hwy 2. It bordered 160th avenue. Picture 2011. (See *Ringgold County 1915 Ogle Iowa Historical Atlas* C. D. Nichols).

We could look out and see them playing in the snow on a moonlight night. They were killing my little chickens in the spring. We got poison and put it on some of the dead chicks and put them around different places. By the time we had started back over the same route we had taken, the rats had gotten the chickens with the poison. One day we got Arthur's dog, Jack, and he and John together got almost 100 rats. They were terrible! When it snowed hard, I could sweep up snow half way across the rug in one room because it came in around the door.

The ground was poor, the depression had hit, and the drought was hard. The second year there (1934), we raised nothing. John went over the cornfield and could not find over five bushels of corn.

THE GREAT DEPRESSION IN RINGGOLD COUNTY

When Sylvia and John moved to the Old Nichols Place in the spring of 1933, the country was entering into nearly the fourth year of the Great Depression. "The Great Depression reached its nadir, some 13 to 15 million Americans were unemployed and nearly half of the country's banks had failed."[128] The unemployment rate by 1933 reached over 24%, compared to just over 3% four years earlier.[129]

THE OLD NICHOLS PLACE

L to R: Paul Lay, Gloria Dickerson, Keith Lawrence[130]

---

[128] "The Great Depression" http://www.history.com/topics/great-depression.
[129] "The Great Depression in Ringgold County" http://iagenweb.org/ringgold/history/misc/hist-depression.html.
[130] It is unclear as to the identify of Gloria Dickerson and Keith Lawrence.

Sylvia wrote that during the spring of 1934, they were able to raise nothing. An article, *The Great Depression in Ringgold County*, supported her description of the difficulties of farming by stating that "the spring of 1934 passed with no rainfall whatsoever. The days of May, June, and July passed with no clouds in sight and temperatures ranging from 105 to 111-degrees. On July 1st, the crops began to burn up in the fields. The rain did come, but on August 30th, much too late to save the crops and pastureland. With nothing to feed their livestock, many farmers were forced to sell off the animals. Some even gave their livestock away. Many farmers turned to the Farm Bureau office in Mount Ayr for assistance in obtaining some sort of feed stuff during the winters of 1934 and 1935."[131]

This may have played a role in Sylvia and John's decision the next year to not only move off of the Nichol's place but also to consider moving out of Ringgold County.

Robert Off to College

During this time, Robert had his driver's license. He got it when John was sick with asthma, so he could drive to school and come home at night. Robert graduated from Mt. Ayr High School (1933). We couldn't pay for the license for the car, so we stored it. Instead, we drove the horses to town the night he graduated.

Robert Lay: High School
Graduation 1933

The next fall (1934), Veda [132] said she would loan Robert money to go to business school. We had made such big plans to send him to college, but

---

[131] "The Great Depression in Ringgold County" http://iagenweb.org/ringgold/history/misc/hist-depression.html.

[132] Veda (Oveda) Lay, John's sister, was born on June 12, 1877 and died on December 12, 1969. She never married.

everything seemed to be against us. We didn't have any money. So he went to Des Moines to AIB College, paying his own way with borrowed money ($200) from Veda; he paid it back when he started to work.

AMERICAN INSTITUTE OF BUSINESS

AIB was established in 1921 in Des Moines, Iowa, meeting originally in Victoria Hotel (photo right[133]) on 6th avenue until 1934. During Robert's first year at AIB , he studied at the Victoria Hotel.

In 1935, the college moved to 10th and Grand in Des Moines (photo below[134]), during Robert's second year at the college.

In 1972, the college moved to its current location on Fleur Drive and changed its name in 2000 to AIB College of Business.

---

[133] Picture public domain.
[134] Picture public domain.

LUTHER CALEB LAY

Luther C. Lay, the father of John Lay and the grandfather of Robert and Paul Lay, died a couple of months before Robert graduated from the Mt. Ayr High School. His wife, Sarah (Irving) had died nearly 22 years earlier. Luther lived with family members near the end of his life in Ringgold County. His obituary is listed below.[135]

"Luther Caleb LAY, youngest son of Benjamin and Mary (TURNER) LAY, was born near Battle Creek, Mich., March 26, 1841, and passed to his reward March 3, 1933, at the age of 91 years, 11 months and five days. He was the youngest of twelve children and the last of his generation. He was left without father and mother at a tender age and usually found a home with Christian friends. He was converted and united with the Methodist church in boyhood and the folks at Eureka will always remember how he enjoyed the fellowship of the church and Sunday school when he lived on the farm and was able to go."

"He and another brother came to Buda, Illinois, in the late sixties and in the spring of seventy-two he came by horseback to Ringgold County, Iowa, where he met and married Sarah Jane IRVING September 10, 1875, and established their home in Washington township, Larole Isabel died in infancy (sic). The beloved wife and mother was called to her heavenly home August 11, 1911."

"There remains to mourn his going Mary PARKER and Corwin LAY, of Buda, Ill.; Mrs. Eric ANDERSON, Homer, Lee, John, Joe and Oveda, all of Mount Ayr; eleven grandchildren and one great grandchild. He has been an invalid for the past three years and when the Lord called he was ready and willing to go to meet the loved ones gone on before."

"We have said goodbye to father and mother,
Together we have rejoiced in this world.
Together we shall rejoice in a brighter world.
They have gone because their work was done.
We toil on because there is something for us to do.
When it is our time to enter, they will come down
To meet us in this dark world of sin and pain,
Where we only meet to part again;
But when we reach the heavenly shore we shall
Meet to part no more.
The hope that we shall meet that day"
Shall chase our present griefs away."

---

[135]Mount Ayr Record News 1933.

Luther C. Lay

Douglas Lay at the Headstone
for Luther and Sarah Lay,
Rose Hill Cemetery,
Mt. Ayr, IA
(2014)

Death of Run Away Model A

We had a model A Ford car we had bought just before we went to Idaho (photo below: sample model A Ford). One day John and I couldn't start the car, so we pushed it over by the pasture gate. He said,

"Don't push it until I get the gate open."

But I gave it a shove and tried to jump in. I couldn't get in, so I grabbed the wheel and was standing on the running board. We hit the gatepost, broke it off, and started down the hill, guiding it as best as I could. As I went past John, who was opening the gate, he tried to jump on too, but he fell off right in a big pile of cow manure. He was a sorry

sight. I guided the car down the hill and stopped in a little ditch. We finally got it started and drove back up the hill and got John cleaned up.

GRANDMA PRATT: 1934

Grandma Pratt died the year Robert left to go to college in Des Moines. She was Sarah Pratt, the mother of Estella, the first wife of Peter Rush, Sylvia's step-father, and the mother of Anna, the wife of Homer Lay, John's brother. Her obituary is listed below.

"She was born on a farm near Jacksonville, Illinois. She spent her childhood and youth on the old farm there. In the spring of 1880, with her husband and five daughters, came in a covered wagon to Ringgold Count, Iowa, and established their pioneer home on the prairie land of Middle Fork township. About at the age of 45, she was converted and baptized and united with the Hickory Grove Advent Christian Church, and remained a truly consecrated Christian until she fell asleep in Jesus on Monday evening about six o'clock. She had a gentle, kind disposition, and was always cheerful and uncomplaining. She was a loving, self-sacrificing mother and a friend to all she came in contact with. She greatly enjoyed attending church and Sunday school and went as long as her health permitted."

Levi Pratt and Sarah Pratt (L) and Estella PRATT Rush (R) (White gravestone)
Hickory Grove Cemetery, Ringgold County, IA (2014)

"Her husband, and Fairy's grandfather, Levi Clark Pratt, died on August 19, 1906. She remained in the county until 1919 when she moved to Mount Ayr. She spent the last four and half years of her life in failing health (1930-1934) at the home of her daughter, Mrs. Anna Lay. Sarah Pratt's daughter, Estella, had married Peter Rush, in 1891. Yet seventeen years later, Sarah's other daughter, Anna Elizabeth, would marry Homer Luther Lay in 1908."

Declamatory Winner

The next year (1935) Mr. Bowman boarded with us and taught at the school. Paul won the County Declamatory Contest that year.

Paul Lay (1935)

12

Don't Look Back

1935-1939

After having lived in Ringgold County for over 40 years, mostly on a variety of farms, Sylvia and John would make one more move—to the capital of Iowa—never to live in Ringgold County again, leaving their farm life behind them.

Des Moines, Iowa   (2014)

Life in the Attic

We thought if we came to Des Moines, Robert could live at home. I thought I could take in boarders and Robert said he could pay $30 of the $40 rent as he was paying that much for room and board. So in November 1935, we moved to Des Moines—not too much to move. We didn't have enough left to have a sale, so we sold what little we had privately. We rented Gene Poor's big house at 2720 High St. (photo below). She had roomers and boarders, so they stayed with us. We at last had a modern house.

Original Home on 2720 High St. Des Moines, IA (2014)

When we got to Des Moines, we had exactly $60 after we paid the truck driver for moving us. It took all of the $60 to buy beds, stove, and other items from Mrs. Poor. We managed to get along without going in debt. In February, John got a job with John Marquart. We lived in a big three story house. We slept in the attic, except in the summer. When it got too hot, we slept in the dining room and put a bed in the front room for the boys. Robert drove the car to work—there was no bus he could go on, and Paul started to Callanan Junior High School.

CALLANAN JUNIOR HIGH SCHOOL

The Junior High, named after James Callanan (photo below), is at 3010 Center St. in Des Moines. It was founded at its present site in September of 1927, eleven years before Paul attended school there. Mr. Callanan was one of Iowa's first bankers. Before his death in 1904, he started a college for teachers, Callanan Normal College, later moved to Drake University, becoming the College of Education in 1921. Paul would later graduate from Drake in 1949 and eventually teach part-time at Drake University in the Accounting Department.

Callanan Junior High School
Des Moines, Iowa (2014)

While Paul attended junior high school here, the school commissioned two murals under the direction of, Grant Wood. The first one, "Nation at Work" was painted in 1936, the first year Paul attended the school. The second year Paul attended (1937), a second mural was painted entitled, "Nation at Play." Each mural was viewed as a reflection of President Roosevelt to prepare young people to participate in adulthood. "Nation at Work" was painted by George Grooms and "Nation at Play" by Glen Chamberlain. Paul would have witnessed the painting of both murals while a student there.[136]

"NATION AT WORK" [137]

NATION AT PLAY" [138]

[136] Callanan Middle School Web Site (www.callanan.dmschools.org).

[137] Callanan Middle School Web Site (www.callanan.dmschools.org).

[138] Callanan Middle School Web Site (www.callanan.dmschools.org).

The Garden House

In November of 1936, we decided we were tired of boarding people. Because the Poor's were wanting back in the house, we rented a house at 904 28th St. in Des Moines. The Poor's bought back the beds, but they didn't want the stove or washer, so they gave us $30 of the $60 we had paid them. I needed the stove anyway and the washer although it was about worn out. I loved the place on 28th. It had a garden and a nice big front yard; the bedrooms and bath were upstairs.

The original house at 904 28th St., Des Moines, IA (2014)

Although John had been laid off during the winter of 1935, he got a job at the Ideal Mfg. Co.[139] in early 1936. That spring, Mr. Moon called me and asked if I would like to work, so I went to work packing flowerpots for shipment. My work was seasonal. Robert was still helping with the rent by working at the lumber yard. Paul was still in same school. We lived there two years (1936-1938).

University Farm

Robert told us he was going to be married, so we thought if we got acreage, we could raise our own food since I was off work. So we rented acreage on University Ave. about 80th street, west of downtown.

The current location of the farm at 80th street and University Ave (2014)

The house here wasn't so bad, but the woman moving out left it so dirty. She had let the pups in the house, and we had to clean crap off the floor. We had no bathroom in the house, and again we had to pump our water from a well. There was no gas to use in our gas stove. We moved in August (1938) on a Wednesday, and Robert was married on Sunday. When John came home from work on Saturday, he said the foreman wanted me to come to work on Monday. Although I had thought I would be home during the summer, Paul

---

[139] Ideal Manufacturing Co made reclining chairs and was located on East 1st street between Locust and Grand, just east of the present Des Moines City Hall.

had to spend most of the summer alone. He raised melons and popcorn to sell.

We were now in the West Des Moines school district, so Paul started to high school at Valley High School in Valley Junction. He had used his own money and bought a bicycle when we first came to Des Moines in 1935. He rode it sometimes to school, but other times we would go past the school and take him on our way to work. We lived there a year and 3 months when we decided we couldn't farm and work away from the farm.

2720 High St. Des Moines, IA
L to R: Paul Lay, John Lay, Sylvia Lay (1935)

Valley High School

The High School was built in 1916 and opened in 1917 at 8th and Hillside in Valley Junction with a student population of 300. In 1923, a Junior High was built to the east of the High School. When Paul started to attend High School in 1938, Valley Junction was changed to West Des Moines and a football stadium and track were built just north of the High School.

Paul, a member of the track team, was one of first students to run on the cinder track where later all four of his sons would run on as members of the Valley High track team. Paul would graduate from Valley High School in 1941 along with Phyllis Bennett. They were married in 1949. All of Paul Lay's children (Tom, Gary, Doug, David) would not only graduate from Valley High School, but they would all attend Hillside Junior High School.

The original building of the High School where Paul Lay attended

Valley Junction

John and Paul came to West Des Moines and tried to rent a house here so Paul wouldn't have to change schools again, but they couldn't find any to rent. Then Robert saw an ad about a house for sale with only $300 down. We came and looked at it, but it wasn't modern—a light bulb hanging from the ceiling, a water pipe sticking through the wall, not even a sink, and again an outdoor toilet in the back yard.

The man came out and tried to sell it to us. I said I wouldn't move into a house that wasn't modern, so he said he would pay to make the house modern and add it to the purchase price. We had bought a cow, and I had raised chickens. We gave the calf to Paul, and he bought some chickens and raised them. The man said he would take all of the chickens (if we had 200) and the cow and calf for the $300 down payment and $15.00 a month. It took Paul's chickens to make 200. So we bought the place at 400 9th St. in West Des Moines. We moved in during October of 1939.

Valley Junction 1900[140]

We just got moved in and John got laid off; he had no work all winter. I was still working at Ideal Mfg., but we managed to keep up our house payments. Paul got a paper route and was paying his own way through school. The house was cold and the paper was coming off the walls. We took all the paper off the entire house and painted the walls after we lived in it a few years. We put in light fixtures and after trying for a number of years to heat it with a coal heater, an oil heater, and then a gas heater, we finally decided to put in a gas furnace.

---

[140] Picture public domain.

400 9th St.
West Des Moines, Iowa (2014)

13

The War Years

1939-1948

It is unclear why Sylvia stopped writing about her life after she had moved to Valley Junction in 1939 and why she picked up her story again in 1949. Regardless, as a world war was raging thousands of miles away in Europe and the Pacific during this period, Sylvia would not be immune from the destructive effects of the war on her life in Valley Junction, Iowa.

Sylvia's grandson, Douglas Lay, picks up the story with several episodes of profound grief experienced by Sylvia during the war and then several stories of great joy celebrated by her during this nine-year period of silence.

(L to R):
Phyllis
Bennett,

John Lay,

Sylvia Lay,

Mary
(Steadman)
Rush

High School Sweet Hearts

Shortly after moving into West Des Moines in 1939, Paul, Sylvia's younger son, would meet and begin dating Phyllis Bennett as students at Valley High School (photo below).

While in school, Paul tried his acting skills out in several school plays (photo below left) and was part of the track team (photo below right) while Phyllis was the typist for the school paper, participated in school plays and excelled as a straight A student.

HONOR ROLL

x x x

Phyllis Bennett Leads With 20 A's

When the smoke of battle cleared away, records of the first semester were examined. Between signed and smudged spots on the pages of the record books many interesting things were found.

Honors for receiving the most A's during the semester go to Phyllis Bennett who has 20 of them decorating her report card

The Spotlight

The Valley High School paper

(1941)

Valley High School Football Stadium (1941)

L to R: Bob Clark, Phyllis Bennett, Paul Lay, Phil Broderick, and Charlotte Waddell

In May of 1941, seven months before the U. S. entered World War II, Paul and Phyllis graduated from Valley, Paul graduating 3rd in his class of 65, and Phyllis graduated valedictorian!

The Draft Notice

Two months after the United States declared war on Japan on December 8, 1941,

Sylvia received notice that her youngest son, Paul, was drafted, spending several months starting in February of 1942 at Fort Francis, in Warren, Wyoming. He would spend time next at the University of South Dakota where he was able to take leave and visit his mother and father and girlfriend in Valley Junction (photo right).

Next, Paul spent time at Camp Ellis in Fulton County, Illinois, and then he was sent to Atlantic City, New Jersey. By 1944, Paul was shipped overseas on the Queen Mary to

London, England where he was stationed during the war at the 160th Station Hospital as a clerk.

Shorting after the surrender of Germany in May of 1945, Paul was shipped to Paris for several months and then Paul completed his service in Germany during the reconstruction until 1946 when he was honorably discharged and returned to Valley Junction.

(L) An artist's drawing of Paul Lay done in Paris in Dec. of 1945.

(R) Paul Lay in England after the surrender of Germany in May of 1945.

During Paul's four years in the army, he wrote an extensive amount of letters to Phyllis back in Valley Junction, letters that were discovered after Paul's death in January of 2011.[141]

The Death Notice

Sylvia's half-brother, Arthur, six years older than Paul, was drafted into the Navy. He was a machinist on the U.S. Northampton.

Sometime during the first of December, 1942, Sylvia and John Lay received noticed that her half-brother was killed in action in the Pacific during the battle of Tassaforonga, Guadalcanal. Arthur Rush was killed in action when the Japanese destroyer, Oyashio, attacked the Northampton with two torpedoes.

Arthur was one of 58 men killed during that attack on November 30, 1942, yet over

---

[141] Paul wrote letters to Phyllis Bennett from Feb of 1942 to August of 1945. Over 300 of them were discovered at the same time as the discovery of Sylvia's narrative after Paul's death in January of 2011. There are plans to publish some of those letters in the near future.

700 men were rescued; the ship sunk the following day. He was survived by his wife, Vivian Viola Rush and his son, Arthur.

Original Picture of the Battleship Northampton April 1942[142]

The Northamtpon, along with other cruiser-destroyers, was ordered to halt the reinforcement of Japanese soldiers on Guadalcanal. On November 30, 1942, three American destroyers made a surprise torpedo attack on the Japanese. After three of the American cruisers were hit, they were unable to continue in the battle.

The Northampton, along with the Honolulu and six destroyers, continued to attack the Japanese. However, near the end of this attack, the Northampton was hit by two torpedoes, ripping an enormous hole in the port side. The blast destroyed the decks and the bullheads. Fire-lit oil spread quickly over the ship, and it began to take on water.

Arthur was most likely killed instantly when the torpedoes hit.

Three hours passed, and the Northampton began to sink stern-first. The ship was abandoned and over 700 sailors were rescued. Arthur was 25 years old when he died. Sylvia was 49 years old at the time of Arthur's death.

---

[142] Picture courtesy of Official U.S. Navy Photograph, from the collections of the Naval Historical Center #NH 97808. The picture was taken in April of 1942. Arthur Rush may have been on the destroyer when this picture was taken.

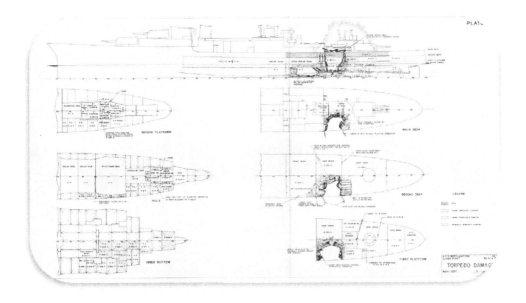

Drawing of the actual torpedo attack on the Northampton[143]

Arthur Lay with his son,

Mary Steadman Rush (Arthur's mother and Sylvia's mother)

Before 1942

[143] Picture courtesy of Mike Green, #0402629 at NavSource Online (http://www.navsource.org/archives/04/026/04026.htm)

In Honor and Memory of Arthur Rush[144]

I recently returned home from visiting the American Cemetery in Normandy, France, honoring the 9,387 soldiers who died in Europe defeating Hitler and the Nazi regimen (photo below).

---

[144] Written by Douglas Lay in 2014.

As I stood in the midst of a sea of white crosses and stars of David, planted above the cliffs of Omaha beach, I was humbled and awestruck at how such a great price and sacrifice paid for freedom was slowly being lost to the next generation. I do not have any memory of Sylvia or her family talking about Arthur's death or his time in the Navy. Perhaps it was my disinterest as a youth about a war that seemed so long ago, or my own lack of memory today as the years press on.

It was a different time then.

Men and women fulfilled their duty, returned home, and continued their lives. My father, Sylvia's youngest son, Paul, served four years in WW II. He returned home in 1946, finished college, got married, and started his family—he was part of the generation called the "greatest generation". Yet, many who served in Europe and the Pacific did not openly talk of the horrors of war—neither did their families.

This should not be.

So, as my grandmother's life is being remembered by her own hand, let us hand off to the next generation the memory of Arthur and the tens of thousands of other Arthurs--men and women who fulfilled the call of the past to preserve the freedom of our future.

Left to Right: Donald Lawrence, Robert Lay; Arthur Rush[145]

---

[145] Donald Lawrence was the son of Fairy (Rush) Lawrence, Sylvia's step-sister.

Rose Hill Cemetery, Mt. Ayr, Iowa (2011)

Unknown Location of the Grave Marker for Arthur Lynn Rush

The Joy of the First Grandchild

The sad news of Sylvia's half-brother's death is shortly followed by the wonderful news of Sylvia's first grandchild, a girl named Karen, in 1943.

Left to Right:

Sylvia Lay,
Karen Lay,
Mary Steadman
Rush,
Robert Lay

Left to Right

John Lay,
Karen Lay,
Sylvia Lay,
Lillian Lay

14

Marriage and Death

1949-1968

Sylvia would write about just a few highlights, loosely strung together covering the next 19 years, beginning with the death of her mother and wedding of her youngest son.

(L to R): Paul and Phyllis Lay and Gloria and Frank Pohlad: Wedding May 15, 1949

A Wedding Interrupted

Mother (Mary Ollie Steadman Rush) passed away on January 1949. She is buried at the Rose Hill Cemetery in Mt. Ayr. She was planning on coming to Paul's wedding on May 15, 1949. Her husband, Peter Rush, died January 4, 1955.

Mary Ollie Steadman (left)   Peter Rush and Paul Lay (right)

Mary Ollie Steadman: Obituary[146]

"Mary Ollie Stedman, eldest daughter of J. S. and Delia Stedman, was born Nov. 23, 1873 in Guthrie County IA and departed this life Jan. 28, 1949 at the age of 75 years. When a small girl she moved with her parents to Ringgold County IA where she grew to womanhood."

"On Nov. 29, 1896, she was united in marriage with Peter Rush and to this union were born seven children: Orville, who died in infancy, Mrs. Hattie Jackson of Red Oak, IA, Mrs. Avis Hetzel of Mt. Ayr; Mrs. Louise Peckham and Mrs. Delia Doser of Melba, ID, Mrs. Lucille Dufresne of Cheverly MD, and Arthur

---

[146] Obituary from paper in family's possession. Submission by Nancy Sackett, October 23, 2015
http://iagenweb.org/ringgold/obitht001/obit_n-obit_r/obit_rushmaryolliestedman.htm

L., who gave his life for his country in WWII. A step-daughter, Mrs. Fairy Lawrence, preceded her in death."

"Early in life Mrs. Rush was converted and joined the Hickory Grove Advent Christian Church of which she remained a faithful member until her death. After moving to Mt. Ayr she and her family attended the Methodist Church where Mrs. Rush was always glad to be of service in any way possible. No wife could have been more devoted to her husband, no mother more loving with her children, grandchildren and loved ones."

"She leaves to mourn her passing the six children, 16 grandchildren, 5 great-grandchildren; three sisters, Mrs. Alice Addison, Los Angeles CA; Mrs. Hattie Geiger and Mrs. Fannie Seaton, Delphos IA, and a brother Leonard B. Stedman, Mitchell SD. Interment at Rose Hill Cemetery in Mt. Ayr IA."

Mary Steadman Rush and Peter Rush
Rose Hill Cemetery, Mt. Ayr, Iowa

PETER RUSH: OBITUARY[147]

"Peter Rush, son of Aaron and Nancy Rush, was born August 9, 1870, in Illinois, and departed this life January 4, 1955 at the age of 84. When a small child, he

[147] Obituary from paper in family's possession. Submission by Nancy Sackett, October 23, 2015.
http://iagenweb.org/ringgold/obitht001/obit_n-obit_r/obit_rushpeter.htm

came with the family to Iowa, where he spent most of his life. He was of a family of 14 children."

"He was united in marriage with Stella Pratt on Sept. 27, 1891. She passed away in 1895. Born to this union was a daughter, Fairy. He was then married to Ollie Glendenning on Nov. 29, 1896 and to this union were born 7 children: Orville, who died in infancy; Mrs. Hattie Jackson of Red Oak, Mrs. Avis Hetzel of Mt. Ayr, Mrs. Louise Peckham and Mrs. Delia Doser of Melba ID, and Mrs. Lucille Harrison of Cheverly MD. Arthur, his youngest child was killed in service during WW II."

"Early in life he was converted and invited with the Methodist church. Surviving are his five daughters, a stepdaughter, Mrs. John Lay of Des Moines, 16 grandchildren, 11 great-grandchildren, two sisters, Emma Elliott and Narcissa Withers of Mt. Ayr IA. Interment at Rose Hill Cemetery in Mt. Ayr IA."

Retirement at Last

John did retire from Western Silo in 1956. I worked for the State Tax Commission for 6.5 years and quit there in 1952. I then worked in a Dime store in WDM and others until I retired.

Golden Anniversary

Last February, 1964, we celebrated our 50th wedding anniversary. Robert, Paul, Lillian, and Phyllis served a lovely dinner they had prepared at the home of Paul and Phyllis (photo below).

This year, 1965, we celebrated our 51st anniversary. All our children and grandchildren and Avis and Harry were here.

John's Hobby

Last September 1964, John fell and broke his hip. He had surgery. He is fine now. He can walk on both feet by holding on the walker. He is painting pictures (photo right).

Closing Words

And June, 1968, we are still living in the same house.[148]

---

[148] These are the last words Sylvia wrote about her life growing up in Iowa.

15

Life After John

1969-1991

Although this is the end of Sylvia's adventures in her own words, written at the age of 74, she would continue to live another 22 years. Sylvia's oldest son, Robert, would continue her story, writing a short update in 1987. Sylvia's grandson, Douglas, would finish her story up until her death in 1991.

Ringgold County, Iowa (2014)

Life after John *by Robert Lay*

Dad (John Lay) died April 7, 1969. Mother (Sylvia Lay) lived alone in the house on 9th street until she moved into a retirement home at 916 Ashworth Rd. West Des Moines Iowa in July of 1985. She will be there two years this July 1987. She sold the house 400 9th to David Lay on July 1985, and he is living there now.

Mother and Dad attended West Des Moines Methodist Church (photo below) while living in West Des Moines (Valley Junction). Mother is living now nearer the church than when she lived on 9th Street, and she usually goes to church with a couple who live at 916 Ashworth Rd.

Mother drove their blue Ford until she gave up her license when she was in her 70's. She mowed her own lawn after that. Lisa (the great granddaughter, daughter of Karen, Robert's daughter) used to tell how in Show and Tell in school mother would tell about her great grandmother still moving her own lawn, and she was past 82.

We celebrated mother's 90th birthday in 1983 at the West Des Moines Church. All her sisters were there. It was the first time for over 30 years that some of the sisters had seen the others. Many friends attended, and it was a nice birthday.

Mother will be 94 this October 31, 1987. To date, Mother had 5 grandchildren: Karen Lay Rhines; Thomas Lay; Gary Lay; Doug Lay; David Lay; and 6 great grandchildren: Lisa Rhines, Robert Rhines, Amanda Rhines, Katherine Marie Lay; Jennifer Mary Lay, and Jessica Erin Lay.

90TH BIRTHDAY—WEST DES MOINES NEWSPAPER ARTICLE[149]

"The 90th birthday of Sylvia G. Lay, 400 9th St., will be celebrated with an open house on Sunday, Oct. 30, in the Fellowship room at the West Des Moines United Methodist Church from 2 to 4 p.m. Friends of Sylvia are cordially invited to join with the family in celebrating this occasion. Hosting the open house will be her sons and wives, Robert and Lillian Lay of Waterloo and Paul and Phyllis Lay of Carroll. Also, her granddaughter and husband, Paul and Karen Rhines of Cedar Rapids and her grandchildren, Lisa, Rob, and Amanda Rhines. Also her grandsons, Tom Lay of Des Moines; David Lay of West Des Moines; Gary and Mary Lay of Allentown, Pa; and Douglas and Tamy Lay of San Juan, Puerto Rico. Mrs. Lay was born October 31, 1893."

90TH BIRTHDAY CELEBRATION: SYLVIA'S HALF-SISTERS
L to R: Sylvia, Hattie, Avis, Louise, Nell, and Dalia

Preparing for Home by Douglas Lay

When Sylvia and John Lay purchased the home on 9th street in Valley Junction in 1939, Sylvia was moving for the 36th time in forty-six years. What she did not

[149] West Des Moines Paper article.

anticipate was that she would not be moving again for another 46 years—living in her only purchased home! After John died in 1969, thirty years after moving into the 1919 built home, Sylvia would continue making 9th street her home until 1985.

At the age of 92, Sylvia would make her 37th move, this time just up the street to Crestview Retirement Home on Ashworth Road and 9th street (photo below). The property on 9th street was purchased by her grandson, David Lay. Sylvia would still live on her own for three more years at the retirement home until her slow decline in health made it difficult for her to live without assistance.

Crestview Retirement Home

In 1988, Sylvia moved to Carroll, Iowa, about 90 miles northwest of West Des Moines, where she would live with her son, Paul Lay, and his wife, Phyllis. Paul and Phyllis cared for Sylvia for about one year in their rental home. Paul had started his own CPA business in Carroll in 1978 (photo below).

In 1989, Sylvia was admitted to the Carroll Health Center, a nursing home, only blocks from Paul and Phyllis Lay's home on 18th street in Carroll. It was her 39th move, and it would be her last one (photo below).

I visited Sylvia in the nursing home while my wife and I were on furlough from Puerto Rico during the summer of 1990. She was still alert and cognitive when we were there. She even joked about the food for lunch that day. My adoptive daughter, Priscilla, had the opportunity to visit with her one last time.

Sylvia's oldest son, Robert, visited Sylvia for the last time around this time (photo below) at Paul and Phyllis Lay's home on 18th street in Carroll. Robert would die in 1990, shortly after this picture was taken.

L to R:

Phyllis Lay,
Paul Lay;
Robert Lay;
Sylvia Lay

(1989)

This is one of many times Paul Lay helped Sylva put on her coat (photo right) at Paul's home before Paul would take her back home to the Health Center in Carroll.

On August 31, 1991, Sylvia Glendenning Lay, after a sudden illness, passed away.

After 97 years and 304 days on this earth, she faithfully closed the door on her explorations on earth and opened the door to her eternal home in heaven—her 40th and last move.

Welcome home, Gram Lay.

JOHN AND SYLVIA LAY

Glendale Cemetery: Des Moines, Iowa (2011)

OBITUARY: SYLVIA GLENDENNING LAY

"Sylvia Glendenning Lay, 97, of 521 W 18th St. in Carroll, and formerly of Des Moines, died at the Carroll Health Center on Saturday, August 31, 1991, following a sudden illness."

"Graveside services were this morning, Sept 3, at the Glendale Cemetery in Des Moines, with Pastor Rod Roberts of the Carroll Church of Christ officiating. Dahn and Woodhouse Funeral Home in Carroll was in charge of arrangements."

"Born Oct 31, 1893, at Ringgold County, Iowa, Mrs. Lay was a daughter of Robert and Ollie Steadman Glendenning. She graduated from Mount Ayr High School in 1911. On Feb. 11, 1914, she married John Irving Lay at Ringgold County."

"She was a retired sales clerk. She had lived in Carroll for the past three years after living most of her life in West Des Moines. She was a member of the West Des Moines United Methodist Church."

"Mrs. Lay is survived by a son, Paul E. Lay and his wife, Phyllis, of Carroll: five grandchildren; nine great-grandchildren, four sisters; Lucille Harrison of Cheverly, Md., Hattie Jackson of Stanton, Iowa, Avis Hetzel of Mount Ayr and Louise Peckham of Nampa, Idaho; a daughter-in-law: Lilian Lay of Clearwater, Fla.; and a brother-in-law, Ray Doser of Melba, Idaho. She was preceded in death by her parents; a son; Robert; and two brothers and two sisters."

Epilogue

A Godly Woman

1893-1991

A Godly Woman

"A good woman is hard to find,
and worth far more than diamonds.
Her husband trusts her without reserve,
and never has reason to regret it."

"Never spiteful, she treats him generously
all her life long.
She shops around for the best yarns and cottons,
and enjoys knitting and sewing."

"She's like a trading ship that sails to faraway places
and brings back exotic surprises.
She's up before dawn, preparing breakfast
for her family and organizing her day."

"She looks over a field and buys it,
then, with money she's put aside, plants a garden.
First thing in the morning, she dresses for work,
rolls up her sleeves, eager to get started."

"She senses the worth of her work,
is in no hurry to call it quits for the day.
She's skilled in the crafts of home and hearth,
diligent in homemaking."

"She's quick to assist anyone in need,
reaches out to help the poor.
She doesn't worry about her family when it snows;
their winter clothes are all mended and ready to wear."

"She makes her own clothing,
and dresses in colorful linens and silks
Her husband is greatly respected
when he deliberates with the city fathers."

"She designs gowns and sells them,
brings the sweaters she knits to the dress shops.
Her clothes are well-made and elegant,
and she always faces tomorrow with a smile."

"When she speaks she has something worthwhile to say,
and she always says it kindly.
She keeps an eye on everyone in her household,
and keeps them all busy and productive."

"Her children respect and bless her;
her husband joins in with words of praise:
'Many women have done wonderful things,
but you've outclassed them all!'"

"Charm can mislead and beauty soon fades.
The woman to be admired and praised
is the woman who lives in the Fear-of-God.
Give her everything she deserves!
Festoon her life with praises!"[150]

---

[150] Proverbs 31 The Message Bible.

ACKNOWLEDGMENTS

Sylvia Glendenning Lay and John Lay

She never could have imagined—long before computers, the Internet, cell phones, and digital photography—that her life experiences growing up in southern Iowa from the end of the 19th century to the start of World War II, would end up as a book. I am, however, profoundly grateful she took the time to record for us about a time in the American heartland that now seems foreign and, at times, unbelievable. It has been an honor and privilege to bring her story to others.

Robert Lay

This project would not have come to fruition without the initiative and diligent work of Robert Lay, (1917-1990), my uncle. When Sylvia was in her mid-70's, he

encouraged Sylvia to record her life story growing up in Ringgold County in southern Iowa. After Sylvia wrote out, by hand, her life story from 1893 to 1968, Robert painstakingly typed out Sylvia's two accounts of her life, on a manual typewriter with carbon paper! Robert is also responsible for much of the initial genealogical records for the Lay and Glendenning families, long before the creation of the Internet and ancestery.com. Robert visited courthouses, libraries, and cemeteries throughout the states and in England, and he wrote numerous letters to family members, collecting additional accounts of his family.

Paul Lay

I am very grateful to Paul Lay, Robert's younger brother and my father. After Robert passed away in 1990 and Sylvia in 1991, he spent time going over dozens of Sylvia's photos, identifying and sharing stories of the family, a number of them included in Sylvia's story. He was proud to have been born in Ringgold County. When I was younger, he often would talk about what it was like growing up in Ringgold, county—I only wish I had paid more attention back then!

David Lay

A special thank you goes out to David Lay, my youngest brother, who trampled throughout Ringgold County with me on numerous fact-finding visits between 2011 and 2014. We took photos of far too many farms and tirelessly explored far too many cemeteries throughout the county, trying to envision what life was like for

Sylvia, our grandmother.

After David returned from serving in the Navy, he would eventually purchase the home on 9th street in West Des Moines that Syvlia and her husband, John, had purchased for $300 down in 1939. He would make a number of renevations, inside and outside. He would sell the house a few years later. It still stands at 400 9th street, turning 100 years old in 2019.

Ringgold County IA Web Project

I am indebted to the folks at the *Ringgold County IA WebProject* for providing an incredible source of information about everything one would ever want to know about Ringgold County. To my surprise, I discovered, on their website, a never before seen picture of my grandfather, John Lay, with five of his seven brothers and sisters and his parents, my great-grandparents, Luther and Jane Lay.

John Lay is the third from the left, sitting on the ground in front of his mother, Jane (Irving) Lay, my great grandmother.

The Lay Family[151]

---

[151] Picture courtesy of IAGenWeb.org/Ringgold County.

Appendix A
The Explorations of Sylvia Glendenning Lay
Time-Line: 1893-1991

	Location	Time	Dates	Events / Chapter
1	James Glendenning Farm	2 years	Oct 31, 1893 to Nov 1895	Birth of Sylvia Chapter 2
2	Peter Glendenning and John Stedman's Farms	1 years	Nov 1895 to 1896	Death of Father Chapter 2
3	Peter Rush's Farm	2 years	1896 to Sep 1898	Remarriage of Mother Chapter 2
4	Montana	6 months	Sep 1898 to Feb 1899	Visit to Grandfather Chapter 1
5	Peter Rush's Farm	1 ½ years	March 1899 to Sep 1899	Orville Dies Chapter 3
6	Old Blauer Place	2 ½ years	Sep 1899 to March 1902	Hattie is born Chapter 3
7	John Stedman's farm	4 years	March 1902 to 1906	Avis is born Chapter 4
8	Peter Rush's Farm	7 years (See #9-14 below)	1906-1914 (Lived 6 other places during this time)	Louise, Lucille, Delia, Arthur Born Chapters 5, 6, 7
9	John Stedman: Delphos	(1 year)	1907 to 1907	Attended Delphos School Chapter 5
10	Aunt Mae and Uncle Leonard's Farm	(3 months)	1908	Babysitting Chapter 5
11	Peter Rush's Farm	(2+ years)	During 1906-1914	Mother pregnant Chapters 5,6
12	Mr. Ayr: Mrs. Dr. Poment	(3 months)	1908	Attended High School Chapter 6

13	Mt. Ayr: Mrs. Webb	(3 months)	1908	Attended High School Chapter 6
14	Delphos: John Stedman	(3 years)	Fall 1910 to Dec 1913	Teaching Delphos and Rose Hill Schools Chapter 6
15	Peter Rush's Farm	(2 months)	Jan to Feb 1914	Preparing for the Wedding Chapter 7
16	Luther Lay Farm	2 ½ years	Feb 1914 to Aug 1916	After the Wedding Chapter 8
17	Delphos: Uncle Sim's House	6 months	Aug 1916 to Mar 1917	Bus Driver Chapter 9
18	Gleason Farm	2 years	Mar 1917 to Mar 1919	Gleason Farming Chapter 9
19	Peter Rush's Farm	1 year	Mar 1919 to Feb 1920	Near death of John Chapter 10
20	Delphos: Peter Rush's Home	3 months	Feb 1920 to May 1920	Recovery for John Chapter 10
21	Oklahoma	2 weeks	May 1920	Recovery for John Chapter 10
22	Wiley House	6 months	May 1920 to Oct 1920	Bed Bugs Chapter 10
23	Luther Lay Farm	6 years	Oct 1920 to Fall 1926	Paul Lay born Chapter 10
24	Mt Ayr: Next to Hattie	6 months	Fall 1926 to Spring 1927	John the salesman Chapter 10
25	Luther Lay Farm	1 year	Spring 1927 to March 1928	Return to the Lays Chapter 11
26	Irving Farm: Tingley, IA	9 months	March 1928 to Jan 1929	In-Law Farm Chapter 11

27	Idaho	6 months	Spring 1929 to Aug 1929	Sick again Chapter 11
28	Mt. Ayr: Kate Primmer	6 months	Aug 1929 to Spring 1930	Return Home Chapter 11
29	Gleason Farm	1 ½ years	Spring 1930 to Fall 1931	Gleason Again Chapter 11
30	Mt. Ayr: Old Long Place	6 months	Fall 1931 to Spring 1932	Keeping the father Chapter 11
31	Miller's Place	1 year	Spring 1932 to Spring 1933	Chapter 11
32	Old Nichol's Farm	2 ½ years	Spring 1933 to Nov 1935	Robert Graduates H.S. Chapter 11
33	2720 High St. Des Moines	1 year	Nov 1935 to Nov 1936	Boarders in the Attic Chapter 12
34	904 28th Des Moines	2 years	Nov 1936 to Aug 1938	Garden Home Chapter 12
35	University Ave and 80th St Des Moines	1 year	Aug 1938 to Oct 1939	Farm Again Chapter 12
36	401 9th Valley Junction (WDM)	46 years	Oct 1939 to 1985	First purchased home Chapters 12-15
37	Crestview Retirement Home: West Des Moines, IA	3 years	1985 to 1988	Retirement Home Chapter 15
38	Carroll, Iowa	1 year	1988 to 1989	Home of Paul Lay Chapter 15
39	Carroll Health Center, Carroll, IA	2 years	1989 to 1991	Nursing Home Chapter 15
40	Eternity in Heaven		Entered August 31, 1991	97 Years 304 days

Appendix B
Grandparents

One of the challenges of retracing Sylvia's life was identifying all of the family members mentioned in her story. Without the help of any living relatives who knew them, it was a pain staking process to uncover her family tree, a process that took over three years!

Sylvia had five grandfathers (two from her family, two from her husband's family, and one from her step-father's family). She had, however, seven grandmothers—a total of 12 grandparents.

Sylvia Lay: Paternal Grandfather and Grandmothers

Peter Cassel GLENDENNING

Sarah ROSS
Louisa HOLLINGSWORTH
Eliza CARPENTER

Sylvia Lay: Maternal Grandfather and Grandmother

John S. STEADMAN

Delia WILLEY

Sylvia Lay: Paternal Step-Grandfather and Step-Grandmother

Aaron RUSH

Nancy Melvina HAMMER

John Lay: Paternal Grandfather and Grandmother

Benjamin LAY

Mary TURNER

John Lay: Maternal Grandfather and Grandmother

Charles Hood IRVING

Mary PUGH

Appendix C
Aunts and Uncles

By far the greatest challenge was trying to identify the numerous aunts and uncles in the story. Without any knowledge of how many there were, it took over three years to discover there were 84, and she had over 100 first cousins, yet I have not discovered all of them.

GLENDENNING FAMILY: SYLVIA'S PATERNAL FAMILY TREE (#14)

Children of Peter GLENDENNING and Sarah ROSS

1. John J GLENDENNING
2. Mary Olive GLENDENNING   Curt ABARR

Children of Peter GLENDENNING and Louisa HOLLINGSWORTH

3. Thomas E. GLENDENNING   Emma GRETTA
                                   Claudia Eve HASS
                                   Blanch M. DYER
4. Robert GLENDENNING   Mary Ollie STEADMAN
5. Sylvia A. GLENDENNING   Abner HOOPER
6. Peter Claude GLENDENNING   HELEN McBAIN

Children of Peter GLENDENNING and Eliza CARPENTER

7. George O. GLENDENNING
8. Fern GLENDENNING   Mr. BLAIR

STEADMAN FAMILY: SYLVIA'S MATERNAL FAMILY TREE (#10)

Children of John STEDMAN and Delia WILLEY

1. Mary Ollie STEADMAN   Robert H. GLENDENNING
                                  Peter RUSH

1.	Hattie Irene STEADMAN	Ed GEIGER
2.	Sarah Alice STEADMAN	J. M. ADDISON
3.	Fannie STEADMAN	Benjamin F. SEATON
4.	Eva Gertrude STEADMAN	Sim C. RICE
5.	Leonard B. STEADMAN	Mae E. RICE

RUSH FAMILY: SYLVIA'S STEP-PATERNAL FAMILY TREE (#28)

Children of Aaron RUSH and Nancy Melvina HAMMER

1.	James Turner RUSH	Mary Jane MORRIS
		C. W. CRUNK
2.	Sarah Elizabeth RUSH	
3.	John Robert RUSH	LeVina BEDFORD
		Gemima E. WARNER
		Sara Warren GUTHRIE
		Nancy Hockett ARNET
4.	Thomas Jefferson RUSH	
5.	Martha Ann RUSH	John Henry MORRIS
6.	Sirestus Marion RUSH	Margaret (Jeda) ANDERSON
7.	Rosetta Alice RUSH	Francis Marion JORDAN
8.	Loretta Melvina RUSH	John Presely JORDAN
9.	Josiah Grant RUSH	Angie
10.	Ella Margaret RUSH	Thomas Jordan BELLAMY
11.	Emma Anna (Ona) RUSH	Allamando ELLIOTT
12.	Peter RUSH	Esther Estelle PRATT
		Mary Olive STEADMAN
13.	Isaac W. RUSH	Jessie May JOHNSON
14.	Narcissa M. RUSH	Marion WITHER

IRVING FAMILY: JOHN'S MATERNAL FAMILY TREE (#16)

Children of Charles Hood IRVING and Mary PUGH

1. Baby IRIVNG
2. Mary IRIVNG
3. Sarah Jane IRIVNG   Luther C. LAY
4. Dorcas Rebecca IRIVNG   Thomas Pringle HENDERSON
5. Alice Martha IRIVNG   William FIFE
6. John A. IRIVNG   Victoria BASTOW
7. Joseph L. IRIVNG   Nellie PRICE
8. Samuel Corzier IRVING   Mary Isabel PARKER
9. George Washington IRVING   Etta Belle McMINN
10. Emma R. IRVING   Archibald D. FRASER

LAY FAMILY: JOHN'S PATERNAL FAMILY TREE (#16)

Children of Benjamin LAY and Mary TURNER

1. Joseph LAY   Died at an early age
2. Marietta LAY   Lysander COLE
3. Cordelia LAY   Mr. VALKENBURG
4. Nancy M. LAY   Silsly PUMMERY
5. Betsy Jane LAY   Sylsbre RUMERY
6. Lewis Abner LAY   Sarah Jane BARRISON
7. Welthy LAY   Died at age 4
8. Eliza LAY   Died at age 10
9. Pauline LAY   Died at age 8
10. Anna LAY   Mr. MINER
11. Abner Lee LAY   Widowed
12. Luther Caleb LAY   Sarah Jane IRVIN

Appendix D
The Glendenning Family Tree

The birth of Sylvia Glendenning brought an end to her Glendenning family tree. Her family tree is traced back to her 14x Great Grandfather, Adam DE GLENDONWYNE. Her family line lasted over 500 years from 1324 to 1893.

The chart begins with Sylvia Glendenning and then traces her family tree backwards. Her father, Robert H. Glendenning, is listed at #1 (Father), then her grandfather is listed as #2 (Peter C. Glendenning), and then her great grandfather is listed as #3 (John, Big, Glendenning), and so forth back to Sylvia's 14x great grandfather, Adam De Glendonwyne. The children are mentioned for each individual along with their spouse. The dates of each birth and death are listed when known along with the location of each. The dates of each marriage are listed when known.

Generation	Father		Children	Mother
	Sylvia GLENDENNING	1.	Robert Lay	John LAY
		2.	Paul Lay	
1	Robert H. GLENDENNING			Mary STEADMAN
FATHER	8/12/1865 Rush Co, IN	1.	Sylvia	11/23/1873 Ringgold Co, IA
	11/2/1895 Ringgold Co, IA			1/28/1949 Ringgold Co, IA

2	Peter C. GLENDENNING[152]	1886		Louisa HOLLINGSWORTH
GRANDFATHER	6/17/1838 Rush Co, IN	1.	Thomas E.	8/9/1846 Gentry Co, MO
		2.	**Robert H.**	
	8/20/1913 Kalispell, MT	3.	Sylvia A.	6/28/1890 Ringgold Co, MO
		4.	Peter Claude	

3	John (Big) GLENDENNING	11/22/1830		Elizabeth CARTER
GREAT GRANDFATHER	9/28/1807 Brown Co, OH	1.	Elijah	8/31 1812 Greene, TN
		2.	Margaret	
	6/27/ 1856 Carter Cmty, Gentry Co, MO	3.	Henry Carter	8/3/1890 Rush Co, IN
		4.	**Peter Cassel**	
		5.	Elizabeth	
		6.	Susannah	
		7.	Sarah Jane	
		8.	John Franklin	
		9.	Francis Marion	
		10.	Theresy	
		11.	Martha Ellen	
		12.	Rachel Amanda	
		13.	Marion	

---

[152] Peter's first wife was Sarah Ross; second wife was Louisa Hollingsworth; third wife was Eliza Carpenter.

Generation	Father		Children	Mother
4	**Henry GLENDENNING**		11/13/1806	**Sarah ASKREN**
	10/25/1778 Virginia	1. 2.	**John (Big)** Mary	11/4/1787 Pennsylvania
GREAT GREAT **GRANDFATHER**	10/19/1855 Glendenning City Rush Co, IN	3. 4. 5. 6. 7. 8. 9. 10. 11.	Jane (Jenna) Richard James Sarah Henry Wilson William Margret Thomas David A.	4/30/1844 Glendenning City, Rush Co, IN

5	**John R. II** **GLENDENNING**		1775	**Jennett WILLSON**
3X GREAT **GRANDFATHER**	3/6/1748 Dunfries, Scotland	1. 2.	John Elizabeth	1776 Ireland
	7/9/1839 Jackson, Brown, OH	3. 4. 5. 6. 7. 8. 9. 10. 11. 12.	**Henry** Eleanor Betsy Janette Jane Margaret Martha William Isabelle Anna (Nancy)	1841/1850 Gentry Co, MO

6	**John GLENDENNING**			**Margaret KENYON**
	1718 Cooper Fifeshire, Scotland	1. 2.	**John R. II** Samuel	1726
4X GREAT **GRANDFATHER**	1797 Culpepper, Virginia	3. 4. 5. 6. 7. 8. 9. 10. 11. 12.	Isaac William James Thomas Joseph Robert Mary Sarah Margaret Peggy Mary Ann	? Pennsylvania

7	**William GLENDENNING**		1716	**Roseanne KIRKPATRICK**
5X GREAT **GRANDFATHER**	5/16/1680 Staplegorton, Langholm Dumfries, Dumbries-Shire, Scotland	1. 2. 3. 4.	Elizabeth John Andrew Jean	1692 Garrell, Kirkmichael, Dumfries-Shire, Scotland
	11/16/1764 Quarterland, Killinchy, County Down, Ireland	5. 6. 7. 8. 9. 10. 11. **12.**	Rose James Charles Thomas Charles William Archibald **John**	1762 Quarterland, Killinchy, Down, Ireland

		13. William	
		14. Alexander	
		15. James	
		16. Thomas	

Generation	Father	Children	Mother
8	**William GLENDINNING**		**Margaret**
6X GREAT GRANDFATHER	1614 Staplegorton, Langholm Dumvries, Dumbries-Shire, Scotland	1. John 2. Adam 3. Andrew 4. John	1650 Scotland
	1682 Gelston, Staplegroton, Scotland	5. Thomas 6. **William**	?

9	**Alexander GLENDONING**	**1564** **1584**	**Alison GORDON** **Nichola HERRIES**
7X GREAT GRANDFATHER	1536 Glendonwyn Parton, Scotland	1. Robert 2. Simon 3. **William**	GORDON B ? HERRIES 1560 Scotland
	1616 Parton, S, Scotland		GORDON D 1569 HERRIES D ?

10	**John GLENDONWYN**		**Elizabeth GORDON**
8X GREAT GRANDFATHER	1510 Parton, Scotland	1. **Alexander** 2. Simon	1550 Lesmoir, Rhynie, Aberdeenshire, Scotland
	1560 Parton, Scotland		1600 Scotland

11	**Ninian GLENDONWYN**		**Katherine MAXWELL**
9X GREAT GRANDFATHER	1475 Scotland	1. **John**	1489 Pollack, Renfrewshire, Scotland
	1541 Scotland		1515 Scotland

12	**John GLENDONWYN**		**Elizabeth SINCLAIR**
10X GREAT GRANDFATHER	1443 Glendonwyn Parton, Scotland	1. Bartholomew 2. **Ninian**	1455 Ravenscraig, Fifeshire, Scotland
	1510 Parton, Scotland	3. Adam 4. Janet	1518

13	**Simon GLENDONWYN**		**Elizabeth Lady LINSAY** **Marjory JOHNSTONE** **Agnes HEPBURN**
11X GREAT GRANDFATHER	1403 Scotland	1. **John** 2. Simon 3. John 4. Matthew 5. Alexander	LINSAY 1415 Glenesk, Angus, Scotland JOHNSTONE 1403 HEPBURN 1410
	1476		?

14	Simon GLENDONWYN			Mary DOUGLAS	
12X GREAT GRANDFATHER	1378 Glendonwyn, Scotland	1.	Simon	1390 Mochrum, Wigtownshire, Scotland	
	1437 Scots Army	2. 3. 4. 5.	Janet John Bartholomew Hawise	1437 Scotland	

15	Adam GLENDONWYN		1373	Margaret De WAUCHOPE
13X GREAT GRANDFATHER	1345	1. 2. **3.** 4. 5. 6.	John Robert **Simon** William Adam Matthew	1358
	1407			

16	Adam DE GLENDONWYNE			Margaret DOUGLAS	
14X GREAT GRANDFATHER	1324 Glendonwyn Parton, Scotland	1.	Adam	1325 Scotland	
	?			1377	

Appendix E
The Lay Family Tree: 11 Generations
January 27, 1967

Robert Lay, Sylvia's oldest son, did extensive research about the Lay family genealogical tree. He first sent a typed letter to his mother, Sylvia, and his father, John, on January 27, 1967 concerning information tracing the first generation of the Lay family to arrive in American. The letter Robert sent to Sylvia is reprinted below.[153]

Dear Folks:

Karen said Chicago had the worst storm (snow) in history. According to the news there were a total of 23 or 24 inches and strong winds. She said yesterday that she couldn't see the house across Duane St. I guess nobody much went to work today. The A &P grocery is nearby so I guess they can walk there to get beans if they need some.

I got a letter this week from a J. Gilbert Lay in Cook Station, Missouri who had written me earlier about knowing I was interested in the Lay family tree. He had asked me a while back to give him all I knew about the Lays in Michigan. He came from the Lay family from the Carolinas somewhere. Anyway he sent me a sheet he had made up for me showing the following: (Though you might be interested). Here is a list of your descendants back to 1617.

1. Robert Lay   He was born in 1617 and came to the US in some year previous to 1638 (This is only 17 or 18 years after the Pilgrims landed in 1620). So he was an early settler for sure. He was married in 1647 and settled in Saybrook, Connecticut. He was born in England, so I am wondering if Lay might not be of English extraction instead of Scotch.

2. Robert Lay   He was born in 1654.
3. Robert Lay   He was born in 1681 (He was an inn keeper)
4. Daniel Lay   He was born in 1712
5. Daniel Lay   He was born in 1738
6. Benjamin Lay   He was born in 1792
7. Luther C. Lay   He was born in 1841
8. John Lay   He was born in 1891

I am interested in knowing more about these people. No information other than above. Don't know what they all did.

---

[153] I have reprinted Robert's letter in its entirety with only a few proofreading corrections.

Robert then typed the following information on the second page of the letter, adding up the total number of children from the first generation of Lays that arrived in America through Luther C. Lay. The first Lay to arrive in America was Robert Lay before 1638 and he married, after arriving in Connecticut, Sarah Fanner (Tully):

From Robert Lay and Sarah Fanner Tully (1647)

35	children through last Daniel Lay family including Benjamin.
12	Benjamin Lay
8	L C Lay

55   No doubt most of these married so there must be several Lays over the country that can be traced back to Robert Lay listed first on sheet attached and related to you! Maybe all the Lays in the US are related like Grandfather Lay told me once.

Well, back to earth now and go home. Beautiful day here and more forecast for Sat. and Sun.

Robert.

Paul might be interested in this. I don't know (or his boys).

Robert then included a 13-page document including details of the above generations of Lays.[154] Parts of the letter are included below:

"There were three brothers who came from England to the states. The eldest was Edward Samuel Lay, then John Lay, sometimes called Sir John, and the youngest, Robert Lay. Edward Samuel Lay was born about 1608 in England. Recorded in Hartford, Conn. about 1640 and died in 1692 in Portsmouth, Rhode Island. John Lay was born about 1610 in England and died January of 1675 in Saybrook, Conn."

"Robert Lay was born in 1617. Recorded in Lynn, Mass. Prior to 1638; he married widow Sarah Fenner Tully in 1647 and moved to Saybrook, Conn. in 1648-49. He died on July 9, 1689 and Sarah in May of 1676. Robert Lay was a person of some consequence in the area of Saybrook, at one time owning 4,000 acres of land and 50 slaves. To quote an early authority, 'This Robert Lay family does not appear to be well written up. John Lay was written up much more.'"

At this point, Robert included the following personal comment: "Hartzell Spence and his wife started a novel dealing with Robert Lay and his activities in and around

---

[154] This document was from a manuscript of Stewart Ward Lay (September 1, 1954) on 488 Castle St, Geneva, New York 14456 and from the book, *The Descendants of Robert Lay of Saybrook Conn.* by Edwin Hill, Boston: New England Historic Genealogical Society. Robert dated the document in 1987.

Saybrook, Conn, but he and she separated before finishing the novel. I had a letter from him in 1986 saying she had all the material but he did not know where she was. In 1986, he lived in Essex, Conn. I had written Mrs. Spence about the information and I thought she might give it to Essex Historical Society, but to date I have found nothing there. When writing the novel, the Spences lived in the old Lay house in Essex. I saw the old Pratt House in 1985 but did not see the Old Lay house. I think, though, it is still there."

The document continues: "Robert Lay came to the Colonies (Lynn, Mass.) prior to 1638. He settled in Saybrook, Conn. in 1648-49. Saybrook at that time was a much larger grant than at present with Essex, Chester, Deep River, and Westbrook later separated from it. The Town records give designation as to the 'quarters' or Indian names. Westbrook or West Parish was known as 'Eight Mile Meadows Quarter' or by the Indian name of Potogaug. Lyme and Old Lyme are on the east bank of the Conn. River as is also the hamlet Laysville, originally settled by the Lays, but in 1954 while on a visit there, Mr. Steward W. Lay found that the last person bearing the name Lay had passed on."

The following chart is a summary of the material found in the document. It covers eleven generations of the Lays, beginning with Robert Lay (1617) the first generation of Lays to arrive from England to America before 1638 in Connecticut.

Sylvia married John Lay, the 8th generation of Lays in this family tree. His oldest son, Robert, had one daughter and no sons, and John's youngest son, Paul, had four sons and no daughters. Paul's oldest son, Thomas, had two daughters and no sons; the next son, Gary, had two daughters and one son; the next son, Douglas, had one daughter and no sons; and the youngest son, David, had no children. So, the eleventh generation of Lays continues through David Lay, the great-grandson of John and Sylvia Lay.

Generation	Father	Children	Mother
1	**Robert LAY**	Dec. 1647	**Sarah Fenner TULLY**
	1617 England	1. Phebe Lay **2. Robert**	
	7/9/1689 Essex Cemetery, Essex, Conn.		5/25/1676 Essex Cemetery, Essex, Conn.

2	**Robert LAY**	**Jan 22, 1679**	**Mary STRANTON**
	3/6/1654 Essex, Conn.	**1. Robert** 2. Sarah	
	1762 Essex Cemetery, Essex, Conn.	3. Mary 4. Thomas 5. Samuel 6. Temperance 7. Samuel 8. Phoebe 9. Dorothy	

3	Robert LAY		Dec 12, 1703	Mary GRENELL
	1/27/1680	1.	Robert	1684
	7/1/1738	2.	Christopher	6/9/1755
		3.	Lydia	
		4.	**Daniel**	
		5.	Jeremiah	
		6.	Phoebe	
		7.	Jonathan	
		8.	John	

4	Daniel LAY		3/15/1712	Anna BULL
	10/3/1712	**1.**	**Daniel**	3/15/1712
	Westbrook, Conn.	2.	James	
	12/28/1782	3.	Asa	3/5/1790
	Westbrook Cemetery, Conn.	4.	Anna	Westbrook Cemetery, Conn

5	Daniel LAY		5/15/1763	Marcey CHAPMAN
	1734	1.	Christopher	12/27/1742
	1807	2.	Nathaniel	12/29/1775
		3.	Jerusha	
		4.	Ann	
		5.	Nancy	
		6.	Infant	
			1/14/1779	Hanna STANNARD (KELSEY)
		1.	Anna	
		2.	Daniel	
		3.	Louis	
		4.	Abner	
		5.	Lovina	
		6.	**Benjamin**	
		7.	John	
		8.	Hannah	
		9.	Matilda	
		10.	Daughter	
		11.	Daughter	

6	Benjamin LAY			Mary TURNER
	10/1/1792	1.	Abner Lee	1796
	10/15/1844	2.	Joseph	
	West Leroy Cemetery, Leroy	**3.**	**Luther C.**	
	Township, Calhoun Co,	4.	Lewis	
	Michigan	5.	Betsy Jane	
		6.	Marietta	
		7.	Anna	
		8.	Nancy	
		9.	Eliza	
		10.	Pauline	
		11.	Cordelia	
		12.	Welthy	

7

Luther C. LAY		Sarah Jane IRVING
3/26/1841 Calhoun Co. Michigan	1. Mary (PARKER) 2. Oveda	3/22/1851 Columbus, Ohio
3/3/1933 Rose Hill Cemetery, Mt. Ayr, IA	3. Homer Luther 4. Abner Lee 5. Joseph A. 6. Luella May **7. John Irving** 8. Corwin Turner 9. Sari I.	8/11/1911 Rose Hill Cemetery, Mt. Ayr, IA

8

John Irving LAY	2/11/1914	Sylvia (GLENDENNING)
11/16/1891 Ringgold Co. IA	1. Robert Glenn **2. Paul Edward**	10/31/1893 Ringgold Co. IA
4/7/1969 Glendale Cemetery, Des Moines, IA		

9

Paul Edward LAY	5/15/1949	Phyllis Irene (BENNETT)
10/10/1923 Ringgold Co. IA	1. Thomas **2. Gary**	7/24/1924 Valley Junction, IA
1/26/2011 Resthaven Cemetery, West Des Moines, IA	3. Douglas 4. David	6/8/2001 Resthaven Cemetery, West Des Moines, IA

10

Gary Edward LAY	6/16/1979	Mary SHERMAN
2/6/1956 Des Moines, IA	1. Jessica 2. Tiffany **3. David**	1/25/1956 Fort Dodge, IA

11

David LAY	2/9/2014	Elizabeth ANDERSON
7/12/1990		3/16/1990

Appendix F
The Rush Family Tree

Sylvia's stepfather, Peter Rush, was a descendent of Dr. Benjamin Rush, one of the signers of the Declaration of Independence. Peter Rush and Dr. Benjamin Rush both trace their lineage back to John Rush and Susanna (Lucas) Rush. As the chart below shows, Dr. Rush is from the family line of William Rush, the 2nd child of John and Susanna Rush. Peter Rush is from the family line of John Rush, the 5th child of John and Susanna Rush.

	1st Generation	2nd Generation	3rd Generation	4th Generation	5th Generation	6th Generation	7th Generation
John Rush and Susanna (Lucas)	William Rush 2nd of 10 children	James Rush 3rd of 5 children	John Rush 1st of 7 children	Dr. Benjamin Rush 4th of 7 children			
	John Rush 5th of 10 children	John Rush 2nd of 3 children	Benjamin Rush 6th of 6 children	James Rush 1st of 2 children	Benjamin Rush 1st of 7 children	Aaron Rush 11th of 13 children	Peter Rush 12th of 14 children

In other words, Dr. Benjamin Rush is the Great-Great Grandson of John and Susanna Rush while Peter Rush is the Great-Great-Great-Great-Great Grandson of John and Susanna Rush.

	John Rush	Susanna (Lucas)
Son	William Rush (2nd of 10)	John Rush (5th of 10)
Grandson	James Rush	John Rush
Great Grandson	John Rush	Benjamin Rush
Great-Great Grandson	Dr. Benjamin Rush	James Rush
Great-Great-Great Grandson		Benjamin Rush
Great-Great-Great-Great Grandson		Aaron Rush
Great-Great-Great-Great-Great Grandson		Peter Rush

Appendix G
Five Generations: Glendenning, Steadman, Rush, Lay, Irving

Listed below is a summary of Sylvia Lay's five family trees. Each of her five grandparents is listed, followed by the children, the grandchildren, and the great grandchildren along with the spouses for each category. Sylvia's paternal grandfather, Peter Glendenning is listed first, followed by Sylvia's material grandfather, John Samuel Steadman, then Sylvia's stepfather's grandfather, Aaron Rush, then John Lay's paternal grandfather, Benjamin Lay, and finally John Lay's maternal grandfather, Charles Irving.

Table 1: GLENDENNING Family

Sylvia Lay's paternal grandfather, Peter Glendenning, was married three times, producing 8 children. His first wife, Sara Ross, had two children. After her death, Peter married Louisa Hollingsworth, and they had four children. Their second child, Robert, was the father of Sylvia. Three years before Sylvia was born, Louisa died. When Robert died five years later, Peter moved to Montana and married Eliza Carpenter. She had two children, George and Fern, both younger than Sylvia—thus Sylvia's two uncles were younger than her.

	CHILDREN	SPOUSE	GRAND CHILDREN	SPOUSE	GREAT GRAND CHILDREN	SPOUSE
	**Peter Cassel GLENDENNING** B 6/17/1838 D 8/20/1913 **(1) Sarah ROSS**					
1	John J. GLENDENNING B 1864					

	CHILDREN	SPOUSE	GRAND CHILDREN	SPOUSE	GREAT GRAND CHILDREN	SPOUSE
2	Mary Olive GLENDENNING B 6/27/1862 D 11/7/1901	Curt ABARR B 11/9/1864 D 5/12/1947	Lela ABARR B 1893			
			Merle ABARR B 1900			

	CHILDREN	SPOUSE	GRAND CHILDREN	SPOUSE	GREAT-GRAND CHILDREN	SPOUSE
	**Peter Cassel GLENDENNING** B 6/17/1838 D 8/20/1913 **(2) Louisa HOLLINGSWORTH** B 8/9/1846 D 6/28/1890					
3	Thomas E. GLENDENNING B 11/7/1866 D 11/16/1938	Emma GRETTA B 1872 D 9/18/1893				

		Claudia Eve HASS (Divorced 1907)	Kenneth Claude GLENDENNING B 5/14/1904 D 7/1968		
		Blanch M DYER B 1882 D 1962			

	CHILDREN	SPOUSES	GRAND CHILDREN	SPOUSE	GREAT GRAND CHILDREN	SPOUSE
4	Robert H. GLENDENNING B 8/12/1865 D 11/2/1895	Mary Ollie STEADMAN B 11/23/1873 D 1/28/1949	Sylvia GLENDENNING B 10/31/1893 D 8/31/1991	John Irving LAY B 11/16/1891 D 4/7/1969	Robert Glenn LAY B 12/27/1916 D 1990	Lillian Eleanor McLUCAS B 2/3/1917 D 1995
					Paul E. LAY B 10/10/1923 D 1/26/2011	Phyllis BENNETT B 7/24/1924 D 6/8/2001

5	Sylvia A. GLENDENNING B 1875 D 1950	Abner HOOPER	Paul HOOPER B 1915			

6	Peter Claude GLENDENNING B 10/26/1878 D 1/4/1943	Helen McBAIN B 10/19/1887 D 4/14/1969	Robert B GLENDENNING B 7/2/1920 D 2/14/1985	Margaret GRAVES B 7/31/1922 D 2/31/1922	Evelyn GLENDENNING	Earl CROSIER
					Charles GLENDENNING	
					Maurice GLENDENNING	

Peter Cassel GLENDENNING B 6/17/1838 D 8/20/1913 (3) Eliza CARPENTER B 9/13/1864 D 2/4/1948						
	CHILDREN	SPOUSES	GRAND CHILDREN	SPOUSE	GREAT GRAND CHILDREN	SPOUSE
7	George O. GLENDENNING B 1905					

8	Fern GLENDENNING	BLAIR				

Table 2: STEADMAN Family

Sylvia Lay's maternal grandfather, John Samuel Steadman, married Delia Willey, and they produced six children. Their oldest, Mary Ollie, was Sylvia's mother. The next four children were girls: Hattie, Sarah, Fannie, and Eva. The youngest, a boy, was Leonard. Eva and Leonard married spouses who were brother (Sim Rice) and sister (Mae Rice).

<table>
<tr><td colspan="8" align="center">John Samuel STEADMAN
B 1/29/1847   D 8/24/1917
Delia WILLEY
B 12/1/1852   D 3/4/1934</td></tr>
<tr><td></td><td>Children</td><td>Spouses</td><td>Grand Children</td><td>Spouse</td><td>Great Grand Children</td><td>Spouse</td></tr>
<tr><td rowspan="9">1</td><td rowspan="9">Mary Ollie STEADMAN B 11/23/1873 D 1/28/1949</td><td rowspan="2">Robert H. GLENDENNING B 8/12/1868 D 11/24/1895</td><td rowspan="2">Sylvia GLENDENNING B 10/31/1893 D 8/31/1991</td><td rowspan="2">John Irving LAY B 11/16/1891 D 4/7/1969</td><td>Robert Glenn LAY B 12/27/1916 D 1990</td><td>Lillian Eleanor McLUCAS B 2/3/1917 D 1995</td></tr>
<tr><td>Paul E. LAY B 10/10/1923 D 1/26/ 2011</td><td>Phyllis BENNETT B 7/24/1924 D 6/8/2001</td></tr>
<tr><td rowspan="7">Peter RUSH B 8/9/1879 D 1/4/1955</td><td>Orville RUSH B 9/25/1897 D 9/14/1899</td><td></td><td></td><td></td></tr>
<tr><td>Hattie RUSH</td><td>JACKSON</td><td>Donald JACKSON</td><td></td></tr>
<tr><td>Avis RUSH B 1902</td><td>Harry HETZEL B 1901 D 1980</td><td>Roberta HETZEL</td><td></td></tr>
<tr><td rowspan="2">Lucille Nell RUSH</td><td>DEFRESNE</td><td></td><td></td></tr>
<tr><td>HARRISON</td><td></td><td></td></tr>
<tr><td>Louise RUSH</td><td>PECKHAM</td><td>Bob PECKHAM</td><td></td></tr>
<tr><td>Delia RUSH</td><td>Ray BASER</td><td>Timothy BASER</td><td></td></tr>
<tr><td></td><td></td><td></td><td>Arthur RUSH B 4/21/1917 D 11/20/1942</td><td>Vivian Viola</td><td></td><td></td></tr>
<tr><td>2</td><td>Hattie Irene STEADMAN B 1881 D 1959</td><td>Ed GEIGER</td><td></td><td></td><td></td><td></td></tr>
<tr><td rowspan="2">3</td><td rowspan="2">Sarah Alice STEADMAN B 1877 D 1964</td><td rowspan="2">J. M. ADDISON</td><td>Donald ADDISON</td><td></td><td></td><td></td></tr>
<tr><td>Ester ADDISON</td><td></td><td></td><td></td></tr>
</table>

[197]

4	Fannie STEADMAN B 1/4/1880 D 12/17/1981	Benjamin F. SEATON B 10/15/1874 D 12/7/1959	Orr SEATON			

			Paul SEATON B 8/25/1904 D 6/3/1991			

5	Eva Gertrude STEADMAN	Sim C. RICE				

6	Leonard Benson STEADMAN	Mae E. RICE	Burt STEADMAN			

Table 3: RUSH Family

Sylvia's stepfather's paternal grandfather, Aaron Rush, married Nancy Hammer, and they had 14 children. The 12th child, Peter, was Sylvia's stepfather.

	Aaron RUSH B 12/8/1826 D 8/27/1896 Nancy Melvina HAMMER B 2/10/1829 D 3/7/1910					
	CHILDREN	SPOUSES	GRAND CHILDREN	SPOUSE	GREAT GRAND CHILDREN	SPOUSE
1	James Turner RUSH B 7/26/1849 D 11/8/1910	Mary Jane MORRIS B 3/6/1852 D 2/21/1931	William RUSH B 1877	Mozel Maud WOODRING		
			Charles RUSH B 1878			
			Lawrence D. RUSH B 9/28/1880 D 12/28/1956	Rebecca L. DUGGER B 12/23/1886 D 3/15/1967	Warren RUSH	
					Russell RUSH	
					Turner RUSH	
					Goldie RUSH	GOODWIN
					Naomi RUSH	COOK
					Norma RUSH	BROWN
	C. W. CRUNK D 1916		Sina Esther RUSH B 6/2/1883 D 11/11/1972	Robert Jordan JOHNSON B 12/25/1878 D 4/17/1978		
			Elwood L. RUSH B 4/5/1888 D 1/17/1959	Ethel Cora GREGORY B 10/1/1890 D 7/19/1963	Velma RUSH	John CARROLL B 8/24/1917 D 2/11/1991
					Grant Ervin RUSH B 9/22/1921 D 12/5/1968	
			Clarence RUSH			
			5 Children died before 1931			
2	Sarah Elizabeth RUSH B 10/26/1850 D 8/4/1851					
3	John Robert RUSH B 1/8/1852 D 11/25/1937	LeVina BEDFORD B 1854 M 1872 D 11/27/1873	Dennis Daniel RUSH B 3/30/1872 D 2/28/1956	Margaret LAHS	Estella G. RUSH B 11/29/1899 D 12/9/1996	Sophus CARSTENS D 9/20/1976
					Esther RUSH	NUZUM

#						
					Ruth RUSH	ZIEMER
					Zella RUSH	HENDRICKS
					Naomi RUSH	LUCKOW
		Gemima E. WARNER B 4/19/1856 M 1880 D 11/9/1883	Lora RUSH B 1881 D 1881			
			Sammie RUSH			
		Sara Warren GUTHRIE B 5/11/1851 M 1888 D 10/8/1907	Martin RUSH Died as an infant			
			Vina RUSH	George STUCK		
		Nancy Hockett ARNET B 1/21/1852 M 1909 D 4/11/1929				

#						
4	Thomas Jefferson RUSH B 11/30/1853 D 11/11/1854					

#						
5	Martha Ann RUSH B 9/17/1855 D	John Henry MORRIS B 6/12/1847 D	Lewella MORRIS B 1874			
			Carrie MORRIS B 1876			
			Corda Bell MORRIS B 5/5/1879 D 8/4/1936	Oliver Miller TAYLOR B 1875		
			Alfred MORRIS B 4/25/1880 D 4/26/1947	Ella	Alfred A. MORRIS B 1909 D 2001	Maude B 1901 D 1981
			George MORRIS B 1882			

#						
6	Sirestus Marion RUSH B 2/23/1857 D 2/19/1943	Margaret Geneva (Jeda) ANDERSON B 12/3/1866 D 10/17/1942	Friend RUSH B 1/1888	Lillian L. MALONE		
			Olive G. RUSH B 5/20/1890 D 5/25/1987	Thomas Jefferson BALLEW B 1892 D 1973		
			Howard RUSH B 1/28/1894 D 1957	Stellia DeFENBAUGH B 1898		

7	Rosetta Alice RUSH B 6/3/1859 D 9/17/1895	Francis Marion JORDAN B 5/8/1856 D 5/20/1923	Nancy Melvina JORDAN B 1879 D 1924	Hans Peter LAHS B 3/31/1872 D 7/27/1953	John Marion LAHS	Eleanor CLARK B 3/30/1901 D 7/30/1932
					Alice Christine LAHS B 5/12/1907 D 10/3/1993	
					Francis Marion LAHS	
			Francis Marion JORDAN B 1880 D 1880			
			Amy Leona JORDAN B 2/12/1880 D 3/4/1886			
			Jessie Gertrude JORDAN B 1881 D 1971			
			Bessie Ines JORDAN B 1883 D 1970			

8	Loretta Melvina RUSH B 10/4/1861 D 6/20/1941	John Presley JORDAN B 5/26/1858 D 3/16/1928	Vera JORDAN B 2/19/1894 D 8/15/1897			
			Mida Lois JORDAN B 10/21/1899 D 7/28/1990	Gerald DORSEY B 5/23/1896 D 4/15/1989	John Grant DORSEY B 12/26/1918 D 12/23/2002	Helen Marie BORGENS B 7/7/1915 D 12/10/2001
					Herald DORSEY B 6/22/1920 D 3/1/2004	Rosina Irene BOLLIG B 2/9/1919 D 5/10/2005
					Ethel Lois DORSEY B 6/13/1923 D 9/1/2000	Sanford LeRoy BEASLEY B 11/16/1917 D 4/28/2004
					Glen Tilton DORSEY B 1925 D 10/22/1949	
					Mary Loretta DORSEY B 2/6/1927 D 12/24/2006	John LEWIS
					Clifford Morris DORSEY B 12/17/1929 D 2/11/2001	
					Gerald Junia DORSEY B 1937 D 9/5/1961	

9	Josiah Grant RUSH B 8/9/1863 D 9/10/1937	Angie B 1867 D			

10	Ella Margaret RUSH B 7/27/1866 D 9/22/1932	Thomas Jordan BELLAMY B 2/26/1857 D 5/6/1930	Earl Chloe BELLAMY		(6 children)
			Dora BELLAMY	CLAYBURG	

11	Emma Ana (Ona) RUSH B 11/17/1868 D 8/1/1963	Allamando ELLIOTT B 1865 D 1946	Florence Modessa ELLIOTT B 4/9/1888 D 9/8/1984			
			Gladys Marie ELLIOTT B 11/20/1901 D 11/15/1978	Rew Tilton KEENAN B 7/29/1894 D 4/3/1959	Albert KEENAN	
					Lee KEENAN	
					Robert KEENAN	
					Carl KEENAN	
					Dorthy KEENAN	
					Jean KEENAN	
					Lula KEENAN	
			Alice Margueritte ELLIOTT B 11/2/1907 D 6/7/1984	Dennis D. TERWILLIGER B 1906 D 1978	Joan TERWILLIGER	Rollin NOBLE
					Sue TERWILLIGER	Richard RUCKMAN
			Mark ELLIOTT			
			Reese ELLIOTT			

12	Peter RUSH B 8/9/1870 D 1/4/1955	Esther Estelle PRATT B 4/13/1870 D 8/5/1895	Fairy Belle RUSH B 10/24/1892 D 2/2/1935	Conrad LAWRENCE B 5/26/1892 D 4/19/1967	Richard Leroy LAWRENCE B 11/22/1919 D 12/23/2003	Laura Eileen PRIVITT B 4/15/1919 D 10/7/2012
		Mary Olive STEADMAN B 1873 D 1949	Orville RUSH B 7/25/1897 D 9/14/1899			
			Hattie RUSH B 2/19/1900	JACKSON		
			Avis RUSH B 12/16/1902	Harry HETZEL		
			Lucille (Nell) RUSH	DUFRESNE		
				HARRISON		
			Louise RUSH	PECKMAN B 12/15/1906?		

		Delia RUSH	Ray BASER		
		Arthur RUSH B 4/21/1917 D 11/30/1942			

13	Isaac W. RUSH B 6/26/1872 M 8/28/1892 D 7/18/194; Ringgold IA	Jessie May JOHNSON B 1/ ?/ 1876 D 5/30/1934	Harry H. RUSH B 1905 D 1913			
			Alta RUSH	COLLINS		
			Ona RUSH	MILLER		
			Percy RUSH			
			Jessie RUSH	TALLMAN		
			Della RUSH B 7/23/1915 D 10/10/2010	Gerald O. SMUCK D 1/24/1992	Ronald G. SMUCK	
					Larry SMUCK	
					Cheri SMUCK	
					Nancy J. SMUCK	
					M. Sue SMUCK	
			Dwight R RUSH B 3/11/1906 M 6/26/1926 D 8/22/1999	Madge E COMBS	Robert D. RUSH	
					Shirley RUSH	Alex ROCCO
			Lyle E. RUSH			
			Clyde A. RUSH B 1918 D 1949			

14	Narcissa M RUSH B 12/15/1874 D 8/31/1958	Marion WITHERS B 1871 D 1954				

Table 4: LAY Family

John Lay's paternal grandfather, Benjamin Lay, married Mary Turner, and they produced 12 children. John Lay's father, Luther, was the youngest of the 12 children.

			Benjamin LAY			
			B 10/1/1792 D 10/15/1844			
			Mary TURNER			
			B 2/7/1797			
	CHILDREN	**SPOUSES**	**GRAND CHILDREN**	**SPOUSE**	**GREAT GRAND CHILDREN**	**SPOUSE**
1	Joseph LAY B 1/5/1817					
2	Marietta LAY B 4/24/1820 D 4/5/1916	Lysander COLE B 10/10/1814 D 7/27/1909	Oscar COLE B 10/31/1839 D 4/5/1911	Elizabeth HALL		
			Alonsa COLE B 8/7/1852 D 3/21/1900	KELSEY	Milla COLE B 1874 D 2/5/1901	
3	Cordelia LAY B 2/10/1822	VALKENBURG D 1855				
4	Nancy M LAY B 2/3/1824 D 12/25/1847	Silsly PUMMERY B 1818 D 1841				
5	Betsy Jane LAY B 12/22/1826	Sylsbre R. RUMERY B 1819	Maria Mary RUMERY B 1848 D 1877			
			Horatio RUMERY B 1852 D 1932			
			Cordelia R. RUMERY B 1853 D 1853			
6	Lewis Abner LAY B 11/16/1828 D 9/7/1907	Sarah Jane BARRISON B 5/12/1834 D 12/18/1892	Homer L LAY B 1858 D 1928			
			Dora J LAY B 1861 D 1914			

7	Welthy LAY B 10/18/1830 D 11/18/1834					

8	Eliza LAY B 2/1832 D 9/21/1842					

9	Pauline LAY B 2/1834 D 7/25/1842					

10	Anna LAY B 7/5/1836	MINER				

11	Abner LAY B12/23/1838 D 9/28/1903	(Widowed)	No Children			

12	Luther Caleb LAY B 3/26/1841 D 3/3/1933	Sarah Jane IRVING B 3/22/1851 D 8/11/1911	Mary Elizabeth LAY B 1/6/1876 D 8/16/1954	Lewis PARKER B 2/18/1879 D 11/2/1951	Louella Grace PARKER B 9/13/1904 D 11/13/1969	Willie FRANK B 3/15/1929 D 5/15/1983
					Mary Pearl PARKER B 2/25/1906 D 6/30/1964	Not married
					Florence Ruth PARKER B 10/12/1910 D 8/17/1994	Leonard CARTER B 3/15/1898 D 5/3/1978
					Gladys Lorine PARKER B 1/13/1913	Howard WILSON B 8/18/1880 D 6/24/1964
					Mildred Jane PARKER B 11/18/1915	Kenneth HERBERT B 11/12/1909
			Oveda E. LAY B 6/12/1877 D 12/12/1963	Unmarried		
			Homer Luther LAY B 8/5/1879 D 10/11/1969	Anna Elizabeth PRATT B 3/18/1879 D 12/1969	Luther Clark LAY B 5/17/1908	Florence RAMER B 9/30/1907
					Wilbur LAY B 4/13/1912 D 9/27/1983	Madelyn KEPLINGER B 10/9/1915 D 11/7/1995
					Blanch LAY	

						B 8/15/1916 D 8/15/1916 (Stillborn)	
			Abner Lee LAY B 4/5/1881 D 1/12/1962	Unmarried			
			Corwin Turner LAY B 3/5/1883 D 3/21/1962	Unmarried			
			Joseph A LAY B 12/5/1884 D 4/23/1959	Unmarried			
			Luella May LAY B 9/19/1887 D 7/14/1954	Eric ANDERSON B 3/19/1886 D 6/1940	Anna Jane ANDERSON B 11/15/1918	Leland DUFFIELD D 4/14/1945
						Carl DeVRIES B 1899 D 7/27/1962
					Helen Luella ANDERSON B 8/11/1921	Elmer C. POORE B 9/12/1920
			John Irving LAY B 11/16/1891 D 4/7/1969	Sylvia GLENDENNING B 10/31/1893 D 8/31/1991	Robert Glenn LAY B 12/27/1916 D 1990	Lillian Eleanor McLUCAS B 2/3/1917 D 1995
					Paul E. LAY B 10/10/1923 D 1/26/ 2011	Phyllis BENNETT B 7/24/1924 D 6/8/2001
			Sarah Isabell LAY B 12/12/1892 D 2/15/1895			

Table 5: IRVING Family

John Lay's maternal grandfather, Charles Irving, married Mary Pugh, producing 10 children. Their first child died at birth, and the second child died at age 12. Their third child, Sarah Jane, married Luther Lay, John Lay's father.

	Charles Hood IRVING **Mary PUGH** B 8/16/1822 D 1/8/1984					
	CHILDREN	**SPOUSES**	**GRAND CHILDREN**	**SPOUSE**	**GREAT GRAND CHILDREN**	**SPOUSE**
1	Baby IRVING					

2	Mary IRVING B 1848 D 1860					

3	Sarah Jane IRVING B 3/22/1851 D 8/11/1911	Luther C. LAY B 3/26/1841 D 3/3/1933	Mary Elizabeth LAY B 1/6/1876 D 8/16/1954	Lewis PARKER B 2/18/1879 D 11/2/1951	Louella Grace PARKER B 9/13/1904 D 11/13/1969	Willie FRANK B 3/15/1929 D 5/15/1983
					Mary Pearl PARKER B 2/25/1906 D 6/30/1964	Not married
					Florence Ruth PARKER B 10/12/1910 D 8/17/1994	Leonard CARTER B 3/15/1898 D 5/3/1978
					Gladys Lorine PARKER B 1/13/1913	Howard WILSON B 8/18/1880 D 6/24/1964
					Mildred Jane PARKER B 11/18/1915	Kenneth HERBERT B 11/12/1909
			Oveda E. LAY B 6/12/1877 D 12/12/1963	Not Married		
			Homer Luther LAY B 8/5/1879 D 10/11/1969	Anna PRATT	Luther Clark LAY B 5/17/1908	Florence RAMER B 9/30/1907
					Wilbur LAY B 4/13/1912 D 9/27/1983	Madelyn KEPLINGER B 1915 D 1995
					Blanch LAY B 1916 D 1916	

		Abner Lee LAY B 4/5/1881 D 1/12/1962	Not Married		
		Corwin Turner LAY B 3/5/1883 D 3/21/1962	Not Married		
		Joseph A LAY B 12/5/1884 D 4/23/1959	Not Married		
		Luella May LAY B 9/19/1887 D 7/14/1954	Eric ANDERSON B 3/19/1886 D 6/1940	Anna Jane ANDERSON B 11/15/1918	Leland DUFFIELD D 4/14/1945
					Carl DeVRIES B 1899 D 7/27/1962
				Helen Luella ANDERSON B 8/11/1921	Elmer C. POORE B 9/12/1920
		John Irving LAY B 11/16/1891 D 4/7/1969	Sylvia GLENDENNING B 10/31/1893 D 8/31/1991	Robert Glenn LAY B 12/27/1916 D 1990	Lillian Eleanor McLUCAS B 2/3/1917 D 1995
				Paul E. LAY B 10/10/1923 D 1/26/2011	Phyllis BENNETT B 7/24/1924 D 6/8/2001
		Sarah Isabell LAY B 12/12/1892 D 2/15/1895			

4	Dorcas Rebecca IRVING B 3/9/1852 D 11/1934	Thomas Pringle HENDERSON B 1850 D 1890	Ethel HENDERSON Died before 1878			
			Ora HENDERSON B 9/14/1878 D 8/1954	Burton CLARK	Ramona CLARK	Louis STATERE
					Russel CLARK	Dorothy LANGDON
			Maude HENDERSON B 1/13/1885 D	Arthur David MASON B 3/28/1886 D	No children	
			Charles Irving HENDERSON B 3/18/1888 D 6/2/1966	Ruth WARNER B 1/30/1897 D 8/9/1986	Donald Horton HENDERSON B 12/24/1924 D 10/15/2007	

5	Alice Martha IRVING B 2/15/1855 D 11/29/1935	William FIFE B 7/8/1861 D 1/1/1923	Baby FIFE / Arthur FIFE		

6	John A IRVING B 2/13/1857 D 11/ 1943	Victoria BASTOW B 18/16/1864 D 3/5/1958	Edmond Burk IRVING B 9/13/1895 D 5/13/1956	Dorothy W WHITTLSEY B 10/28/1915 D 12/12/1998	John Albert IRVING B 10/5/1949 D 1/11/1954	
			George Oliver IRVING B 10/25/1899 D 1982	Marjorie RITZ B 12/21/1899 D 11/26/1985	David Julian IRVING B 12/28/1926 D 1/8/2014	Darlene DULANY
			John IRVING B 1901 D 1994	Florence JUERGENS B 1901 D1981	Anna Lynn IRVING B 4/13/1936	Harry Curtis BEVINGTON B 11/8/1935

7	Joseph L. IRVING B 11/26/1859 D 8/17/1949	Nellie PRICE B 1/28/1876 D 4/3/1951	Hugh IRVING B 1903 D 1972	Fern TYRRELL B 1903 D 1972	Jay IRVING / Shirley IRVING	
			Florence Mary IRVING B 9/10/1906 D 10/23/1981	Ernest MERCER B 1/12/1905	Leslie MERCER B 7/30/1930	Minna Lou SCHARMAN
					Donald Eugene MERCER B 4/10/1932	Mary Ruth WILLIAMS
					Robert Keith MERCER B 3/24/1933	Sonja Salyer
					Eleanor Kay MERCER B 11/19/1941	George PRATT
			Sewell IRVING			
			Joseph IRVING			

8	Samuel Crozier IRVING B 7/19/1861 D 6/1/1934	Mary Isabel PARKER B 1865 D 10/ 1947	No Children		

9	George Washington IRVING B 1/8/1864 D 5/6/1947	Etta Belle McMINN B 2/11/1878 D 10/4/1951	Mary Louise IRVING B 12/13/1911	William J. LINK B 1/22/1911	No Children	
			Alice Isabell IRVING B 1/18/1914 D 8/3/1995	David Hubert ALLEN B 2/28/1908 D 2/20/2004	Robert ALLEN B 3/15/1944	Barbara SACKETT B 2/17/1944
					Arthur Lewis ALLEN B 3/21/1948	Nancy Lee SHEPHERD B 1/23/1948

					Ruth Etta ALLEN B 7/10/1951	John ZAHNER
					John David ALLEN B 7/3/1954	Cindy
			Emma Francis IRVING B 7/2/1917	Marvin Travers BROWN B 7/22/1914	Judith Lee Ann BROWN B 9/12/1941	Rev. Bruce BURCH
					Michael James BROWN B 7/10/1944	Vicki JONES (Divorced)
						Betty

10	Emma R. IRVING B 9/27/1867 D 9/1939	Archibald D. FRASER B 8/?/? D 11/ 1940	No Children			

Editor: Douglas Lay

I am a native of West Des Moines, Iowa, and the grandson of John and Sylvia Lay. I grew up living less than 2 miles from my grandmother, Sylvia Lay.

I remember countless visits to the house on 9th street for lunch on Sundays with my parents and three brothers, Tom, Gary, and David. Sylvia is the one who introduced us to sweet tea, and she always had a jar full of chocolate chip cookies waiting for us on the kitchen table.

I spent many summer days mowing her yard and winter days shoveling the sidewalks around her house. My brothers, when we were younger, would often play in the backyard, often in the shed my grandfather had built next to the separate garage in the alley behind the house. We would climb on the roof of the shed to get to the alley or climb through the window in the shed, all the while trying not be seen by our grandmother!

It was not unusual to find her working on the latest quilt she was sewing. She made sure that all of her grandchildren had several of her quilts; the most famous ones were her "state bird" quilts.

When I was in college, I would stop by to see how she was doing when I was home on break. I remember many times sitting down and playing Triominos with her or playing cards. On one particular evening, while we were playing some game, I was unaware that back at my home on 32nd street, my younger brother had called the fire department because his bedroom was on fire!

I was ten years old when her husband, my grandfather, John Lay, suddenly died of a heart attack in 1969. I remember my father telling me the news in our kitchen after coming home from school. It was the first funeral I remember attending of a family member.

Sylvia would live into my early 30's, so I still have vivid and very fond memories of her. She made it a point to treat her grandchildren the same. It was hard to know who her favorites were. She made us all feel loved and welcomed.

She was able to attend my wedding in 1982, and she was able to visit with my adopted daughter in 1990 before Sylvia passed away the next year.

I regret not being able to attend her funeral; I was out of the country in 1991, but working on this book for the past four years has been a blessing and the best way that I know to honor and to remember my grandmother, Sylvia Glendenning Lay.

Other Books by Douglas Lay

Lay, Douglas. *Journey of Discovery: Research Writing in College*. CreateSpace Independent
Publishing Platform, 2013.

Lay, Douglas. *The Irony of Teaching Truth.* CreateSpace Independent Publishing Platform,
2015.

Made in the USA
Monee, IL
19 April 2023

32117669R00129